Ernest Howard Crosby

Plain Talk in Psalm And Parable

Ernest Howard Crosby

Plain Talk in Psalm And Parable

ISBN/EAN: 9783744760928

Printed in Europe, USA, Canada, Australia, Japan

Cover: Foto ©Thomas Meinert / pixelio.de

More available books at **www.hansebooks.com**

PLAIN TALK
IN PSALM & PARABLE

BY

ERNEST CROSBY

BOSTON
SMALL, MAYNARD & COMPANY
1899

Dedication ❧

HAIL, Tolstoy, bold, archaic shape,
    Rude pattern of the man to be,
From 'neath whose rugged traits escape
    Hints of a manhood fair and free.

I read a meaning in your face,
    A message wafted from above,
Prophetic of an equal race
    Fused into one by robust love.

Like some quaint statue long concealed,
    Deep buried in Mycenæ's mart,
Wherein we clearly see revealed
    The promise of Hellenic art,

So stand you; while aloof and proud,
    The world that scribbles, prates, and frets
Seems but a simpering, futile crowd
    Of Dresden china statuettes.

Like John the Baptist, once more scan
    The signs that mark the dawn of day.
Forerunner of the Perfect Man,
    Make straight His path, prepare the way.

The desert too is your abode,
    Your garb and fare of little worth;
Thus ever has the Spirit showed
    The coming reign of heaven on earth.

5

Dedication

Not in kings' houses may we greet
The prophets whom the world shall bless,
To lay my verses at your feet
I seek you in the wilderness.

Contents ❧

Contents

Contents

Contents

Fiat Lux ❧

I

WHO are we that we challenge society to its
face?
Is society irresistible? So are we in our place
irresistible;
The infinite forces of nature work through us;
The narrow past flows on to the broad future
through us;
If we but strive to keep abreast of God's will, God
acts through us.
Who then has a higher right than ours to mould the
world that is to be?

II

But we would not lift a finger against your old-time
contrivances;
We lift no finger and we persuade others as well to
lay aside their weapons.
We dedicate the sabre and musket to a shelf in the
museum above the rack and thumbscrew,
And we know that ere long the ballot-box and
policeman's club will follow them.

Fiat Lux

You could conquer us if we relied on armed bat-
talions or mere majorities,
But we know how to fight the owls and bats of
social superstition;
We have no use for guns;
He that taketh the sword shall perish by the
sword;
We only turn on the light of truth, and all the
dismal hosts flee blindly before us;
We kindle the fire of love, and all are consumed.

III

Gone, soon will be gone, the sham honesty which
lives on others' labour;
Gone the sham authority which rests upon violence;
Gone the sham respectability which is propped up
by privilege;
Gone the sham wealth which is drawn from others'
poverty;
Gone the sham religion which covers the other
shams with its threadbare cloak of hypocrisy.
The night is far spent, the day is at hand;
Already the nocturnal birds and beasts are slinking
into the darker corners.
Soon the Sun of Righteousness will arise with healing
in His wings:
Thank God that even through us His rays may be
dimly refracted!

Truth ❧

I

OUR highest truths are but half-truths.

Think not to settle down for ever in any truth.

Make use of it as a tent in which to pass a summer night, but build no house of it, or it will be your tomb.

When you find the old truth irksome and confining,

When you first have an inkling of its insufficiency, and begin to descry a dim counter-truth looming up beyond,

Then weep not, but give thanks.

It is the Lord's voice, whispering, " Take up thy bed and walk."

II

The truth is one with the way and the life ;

It is the climbing, zigzag road which we must travel ;

It is the irrepressible growth which we must experience.

Hail the new truth as the old truth raised from the dead ;

Hail it, but forget not that it too will prove to be a half-truth ;

For sooner or later we shall have to dismiss it also at another and loftier stage of our journey.

13

Contrasts in Black and White ❧

I

THIS is a mad world.
    The great church is crowded.
The ancient torn battle-flags are hung high on the
    walls, where the dusty red and yellow rays
    from the stained windows strike them.
The monuments of generals who died fighting look
    down at the multitude, among whom we see
    here and there uniformed soldiers from the
    garrison.
And the priest drones: "But I say unto you, Love
    your enemies, do good to them that hate you;
    and whosoever shall smite thee on thy right
    cheek, turn to him the other also."
Yet no one smiles—but the devil.

II

This is a mad world.
In the congregation are great land-owners and
    millionaires, statesmen and magistrates.
They sit content, and the rest admire them and
    would be as they are.
And now the organ peals forth, and the choir sings
    gloriously:

14

" He hath put down, He hath put down the mighty
from their seats, and the rich, the rich, He
hath sent empty away."

And once more the priest reads: " It is easier for a
camel to go through the eye of a needle, than
for a rich man to enter into the kingdom of
God "; and again, " Ye know that the princes
of the Gentiles exercise dominion over them,
and they that are great exercise authority
upon them, but it shall not be so among you."

Yet no one smiles—but the devil.

III

This is a mad world.

The great and learned judge is on the bench.

The throng is silent as the clerk administers the
solemn oath to the witnesses.

The witness swears and kisses the Book;

And in the Book is written, " Swear not at all," and
" Judge not that ye be not judged."

Yet no one smiles—but the devil. ‿

IV

This is a mad world.

The heroes have met together to proclaim liberty.

They have just signed the great charter which
declares that all men are created equal, and
that they are endowed by their Creator with

the inalienable right to life, liberty, and the
pursuit of happiness.

Many of these men have slaves on their plantations
at home, and the slave-trade is prospering.

Yet no one smiles—but the devil.

V

This is a mad world.

For many long years the foreign slave-trade will go
on, while men shout "freedom."

For many years longer men will buy and sell their
fellows, and still shout "freedom."

And after the word "slave" has been abolished,
still for many long years will men oppress
their fellows and rob them of an equal chance
to live, and still shout "freedom."

Yet no one smiles—but the devil.

Morituri Salutamus [1]

I

HAIL, Custom, we, about to die, salute thee!
Behold us, thy slaves and prisoners,
Bound and swathed in ponderous frock-coats and
satin linings, in new-creased trousers, in

---

[1] The reader will note here and elsewhere the indebtedness of the
author to Edward Carpenter's admirable Essays.

starched cambric shirts and silken under-
clothing;

Shackled in stiff collars and wristbands, in gold
chains and finger-rings;

Helpless in patent leather boots, tight-fitting gloves,
and hard-rimmed top-hats;

Decorated, like victims for the sacrifice, with flowers
in button-hole, and rich scarves and jewelled
scarf-pins;

Forced to talk and to walk, to get up and sit down
thus and so;

Made to eat and drink all the unwholesome confec-
tions and concoctions of East and West;

Shut out from the corn-field and market-garden and
workshop, where men really live;

Doomed to lifelong impotence by a thousand irre-
vocable laws;

All man's work done for us whether we will or no;

Forbidden to clean our own boots or put on our own
overcoats;

Guarded by despotic butlers and valets and housemaids;

Looking out of our windows, hopelessly bored, at
the genuine life going by in which we may
not share;

Yawning listlessly in stifling rooms;

Weighed down with aimless bric-a-brac and rugs,
with redundant easy-chairs, picture frames,

2   17

Morituri Salutamus

and upholstery, with all sorts of dust-gather-
ing rubbish;
Our women even more deeply sunk in the glittering
slough than ourselves;
Nerves snapping, digestion spoiled, temper irretriev-
ably lost, soul unheard from this many a long
year!

II

Hail, Custom, we, about to die, salute thee!
About to die? Nay, we are dead already;
These splendid halls are our sepulchre.
All here is death, and the life is make-believe;
These are but pictures of life traced on the walls for
the eye-sockets of mummies to stare at in the
eternal dark.
We are bound hand and foot, and laid in a gilded
sarcophagus;
We strain at ankle and knee, at wrist and elbow, but
in vain;
We would move our lips, but our tongue cleaves to
the roof of our mouth.
Death, death, death; there is a smell of frankincense
and spices, but under it all we are rotting
slowly away.
Oh for a breath of mountain air, an hour of God-
given out-door toil!
Oh for a voice of command from heaven, crying,
"Lazarus, come forth!"

18

Education 🙠

HERE are two educated men.
   The one has a smattering of Latin and
      Greek ;
The other knows the speech and habits of horses
      and cattle, and gives them their food in
      due season.
The one is acquainted with the roots of nouns and
      verbs ;
The other can tell you how to plant and dig potatoes
      and carrots and turnips.
The one drums by the hour on the piano, making
      it a terror to the neighbourhood ;
The other is an expert at the reaper and binder,
      which fills the world with good cheer.
The one knows or has forgotten the higher trigo-
      nometry and the differential calculus ;
The other can calculate the bushels of rye standing
      in his field and the number of barrels to buy
      for the apples on the trees in his orchard.
The one understands the chemical affinities of
      various poisonous acids and alkalies ;
The other can make a savoury soup or a delectable
      pudding.
The one sketches a landscape indifferently ;

Our Charities

The other can shingle his roof and build a shed for
     himself in workman-like manner.
The one has heard of Plato and Aristotle and Kant and
     Comte, but knows precious little about them ;
The other has never been troubled by such know-
     ledge, but he will learn the first and last
     word of philosophy, " to love," far quicker, I
     warrant you, than his college-bred neighbour.
For still is it true that God hath hidden these things
     from the wise and prudent and revealed them
     unto babes.
Such are the two educations :
Which is the higher and which the lower ?

Our Charities ❧

I

YE purveyors of charities ! ye members of society's
     ambulance corps !
Are the wounded and disabled too many for you ?
Is the battle of life taxing your resources beyond
     your strength ?
Do you cry for more money, more asylums, more
     societies ?
Stay for a moment, long enough to think, to break
     the truth to yourselves, and then to announce
     it to the world.

Be frank, and admit that your task is rapidly out-
stripping your ability.

Turn to your rich supporters, and tell them that they
are creating paupers too fast for their gifts
to catch up with them;

That annual subscriptions and soup-tickets and
Sunday church - going are of no use except
to quiet consciences which ought to be
goaded;

That all their Societies for the Prevention of Charity
—of real personal charity—are deferring the
coming of the kingdom of God;

That the only way to stop poverty is to stop
manufacturing it by privilege and covetousness;

That the only way to relieve the ambulance corps is
to order a halt in the battle.

II

Ye purveyors of alms!

Acknowledge once for all the bankruptcy of Organ-
ised Charity.

You know that you are insolvent; that you cannot
meet the demands made upon you;

That many an honest unemployed man asks you for
work in vain, and that his just claim goes to
protest.

At least you can do one thing with him:

Medice, Cura Te Ipsum

Make him a living epistle, read of all men;
Bring his existence home to your distant and deaf
  subscribers;
Do not bury him in annual reports and abstract
  statistics;
Give room in your hearts to the indignation that you
  ought to feel,
And give vent to it boldly in the face of those who
  pay your stipends.
You cannot do better than quote Isaiah to them:
" Thus saith the Lord,
Away with your new moons and sabbaths and call-
  ing of assemblies.
The spoil of the poor is in your houses.
What mean ye that ye beat My people to pieces and
  grind the faces of the poor? saith the Lord
  God of Hosts."

Medice, Cura Te Ipsum ❧

I

PITY our dilettante literary men and artists,
  Cut off from their base of supplies, the
    common people,
Starving, as it were, in a foreign land;
Uttering trim futilities for each other's edification,
Their prophetic function all forgotten.

Medice, Cura Te Ipsum

Such were not the men of old—

Sophocles and Euripides, when all Athens watched
from sunrise to sunset the destiny of Œdipus
or Orestes ;

And Cimabue, when the populace of Florence bore
his Madonna of the dawn in triumph from his
studio to the altar.

Such were not the great musical composers of
our own time, for they too spake for the
masses ;

And to-day, where German workmen meet together,
you may hear sung the noblest chorals,

And the forlornest Italian village can appreciate
Verdi and Mascagni.

The artist must embrace his lowliest fellow-man ; in
vain will he seek for inspiration elsewhere.

The bard and the painter should be the head and
right arm of the people ;

What can we expect from Art when we lop these
from the trunk ?

II

Pity our drawing-room reformers,

Isolated as they too are from the nation's life—

Physicians trying to cure the body politic of bribery
and corruption,

But not probing deep enough to know that the root
of both is the haste to get rich ;

Medice, Cura Te Ipsum

Tainted themselves unconsciously by the same contagion,

Blind to their own symptoms—speculation, monopoly, and caste;

Ignorant that the real foe is not Tammany but Mammony.

There are the good women, too, who long to vitalise our common schools,

And yet overlook the obvious first step—to send their own children to them.

And all those innumerable "mote" societies, bent on making other people behave themselves,

But failing to see that one honest association for the eradication of beams could outstrip them all in usefulness.

Physician, heal thyself.

Reformers, feel the vulgar blood of humanity flow in your veins; it is there, if you but knew it.

Make yourselves one with the people, and they will be whole.

You can only draw health and strength from the heart of the nation;

What are we to expect of your reforms if you respond not to its pulse-beat?

Ye Pharisees

YE Pharisees that rule the land
　　In politics and trade;
Ye money kings, whose least command
　　The world has long obeyed;

Ye portly millionaires, who choose
　　To live in pious style,
Whose bald heads punctuate the pews
　　Far up the middle aisle;

Ye that suck ground-rents from the soil,
　　Ye usurers of the banks,
Who love to live on others' toil,
　　And to the Lord give thanks;

Ye corporation lords, who mock
　　The forms the law allows,
And know the way to water stock
　　With sweat of others' brows;

Ye priests, that utter lies serene
　　To lull the like of these,
And make the words of Jesus mean
　　What you and Mammon please,

Ye Pharisees

Go to the Sacred Book, and see
    The words to you addressed;
To you He saith not, " Come to Me,
    And I will give you rest."

But rather, " Woe to you, O rich !
    Ye blind that lead the blind
Until ye stumble in the ditch
    Where perish human kind.

" Ye hypocrites, that cannot read
    The signals of the times;
Who know not that the age of greed
    Is doomed, with all its crimes.

" Go, tithe your mint and rue again,
    And keep your Sabbath day;
But justice, love of fellow-men,
    And mercy, where are they?

" The orphan's and the widow's share
    Ye hasten to devour,
What if ye bow your heads in prayer
    And mumble by the hour.

" Ye do your alms that all may look
    And note the action fine;
High on the year's subscription book
    Your names are sure to shine.

Ye Pharisees

"And when men meet for this and that,
  Ye love the upper seat;
For you, to see them lift their hat
  And stare at you is sweet.

"Ye lawyers of the senate hall,
  And ye of bench and bar,
The burthens of your statutes fall
  Where'er the poorest are.

"Not with one finger will ye aid
  To ease your neighbour's task;
If rent and interest be paid,
  This, this is all ye ask.

"The key of knowledge, lo, ye hide,
  Nor let your fellows know
That love alone can turn the tide
  Which buries them in woe.

"Behold the monuments ye build
  To them your fathers stoned!
And so the seers ye would have killed
  Ere long will be enthroned.

"Fit sons of those who used to trade
  In flesh of ebon hue,
Ye think that white and black were made
  To moil and toil for you.

Ye Pharisees

"And them that would their country rid
    Of every kind of slave,
Ye treat them as your fathers did,
    And slander those who save.

"Ye whited sepulchres, that loom
    So stately to the eye,
Down in the bottom of the tomb
    All filth and foulness lie.

"And think ye then that such as ye
    God's reign on earth may view?
The tramp and prostitute will be
    More welcome there than you."

So speaks your Testament.   Take heed,
    Ye that have ears to hear;
Accept this lesson as you read—
    Repent.   God's reign is near.

And now, while still your choice is free,
    Against your god rebel—
Your god, respectability,
    The dullest fiend in hell.

His Message ❧

I

HE came with good tidings, it is true,
  But they were good tidings only to the poor.
For us, who are content to be rich while our
  brethren suffer want,
There was not one word of cheer in all His message.

II

"Come unto Me, and I will give you rest," was His cry,
But He addressed it only to them that "labour and
  are heavy laden."
To us, who have never done for a single day our
  share of the work of the world,
There comes no such invitation.

III

But He had words for us also;
We too must hear Him speak, but from another
  standpoint.
Let us take our proper place in the group of scorn-
  ful, self-satisfied scribes and Pharisees who
  stand aloof over against Him.
From that post let us listen to His burning eloquence,
And find a new and truer life and power in His
  language.

IV

We can claim no more than this;
Neither may we take to ourselves His expressions of sympathy and love,
Nor recline with our head upon His bosom,
Until with Him we make ourselves equal with the least,
And accept gladly the common suffering, the privation, and the toil.

The Egyptians

I

WHAT does Moses think of the Egyptian folk as he treads the streets of Memphis and walks out into the great necropolis?
"O most religious of people, anxious for nought but the preparation of your bodies for the resurrection,
Building tombs that will astound the ages,
Pyramids that rival the everlasting hills,
Content to paint your marvellous pictures on the sepulchres' inner walls for the pleasure of the dead,
A whole class devoted to embalming of bodies, pouring in the costliest spices, binding up

with the choicest linen, laying them in magni-
ficently decorated and inlaid sarcophagi,
Burying with them gold and silver and gems, and
the most beautiful glass and pottery,
Preserving the body that you may preserve the soul,
The whole people crying out as one man, 'What
must I do to be saved?'
The energies which other races turn towards the
present absorbed by you in the all-engrossing
life to be."

II

" And this religion of yours, how does it touch your
hearts?
The workmen on your monuments and temples die
like flies in the summer sun, and who cares?
You set taskmasters over them to afflict them with
burdens, and make them serve with rigour;
You make their lives bitter with hard bondage, in
mortar and in brick and in all manner of
service in the field, forcing them to make
their bricks without straw.
Your gaze is so fixed on heaven that you cannot see
the earth;
You are so bent on future happiness that you have
no eyes for the misery you create about you;
Your faith is a mockery and your heaven will be a
hell."

31

The Egyptians

And when the Spirit of the Lord came upon Moses,
    that he gave the law to the people,
How he revolted from the narrow Egyptian creed!
How he directed their minds away from selfish care
.   for salvation in the world to come, and turned
    them towards their duties of to-day.
" Hear, O Israel, The Lord our God is one Lord,
And thou shalt love the Lord thy God with all
    thine heart, and with all thy strength, and
    with all thy soul, and with all thy might.
He doth execute the judgment of the fatherless
    and widow, and loveth the stranger, in giving
    him food and raiment; love ye therefore the
    stranger, for ye were strangers in the land of
    Egypt.
And thou shalt love thy neighbour as thyself."
And though he was learned in all the learning of the
    Egyptians, yet not one word does he utter in
    all his five long books regarding the world to
    come,
Lest the children of Israel should be enslaved by it
    as were the people of the Nile.
And it was from this seed of Moses that sprang the
    flower of Galilee in due time,
To make earth a garden and begin the kingdom of
    heaven here.

Not the Lord ⌒

I

PRAISE ye the Lord,
    For He hath given to His poor a world
    stored with all riches:
Stone in the mountain, brick in the field, timber in
    the forest to build them their houses;
Wool and cotton to make them clothing;
Corn and fruit and every manner of plant for their
    food.
Who hath shut them out from the fullest enjoyment
    of all these things which they themselves
    produce?
It is not God.   Praise ye the Lord.

II

Praise ye the Lord,
For He hath given to His poor brains, and eyes and
    ears of the best,
So that they might know the beauty of the land-
    scape,
So that they might acknowledge the sway of the old
    masters of art,
And feel the thrill of the noblest music,
And take to their bosom the greatest poets,
And love their books as themselves.

3   33

A Psalm for the Poor

Who hath shut them out from all this fruition ?
It is not God.   Praise ye the Lord.

III

Praise ye the Lord,
For He hath given to His poor hearts to love their
    fellows,
So that they might have the key to the kingdom of
    heaven.
Who is it that taketh away the key and shutteth up
    the kingdom against them ?
That neither goeth in himself nor suffereth them
    that are entering to go in ?
It is not God.   Praise ye the Lord. ✓

A Psalm for the Poor ❧

I

THEY speak of brotherhood ;
    They say that we are all brethren ;
That we have one Father in heaven, who is no
    respecter of persons and before whom we are
    all equal ;
But their life is a lie.
    O Lord, how long ?

34

A Psalm for the Poor

They discourse of love ;
They tell us how their hearts go out to us ;
They point to their great charities, and who can
  deny the proofs of brick and mortar and hard
  red gold ?
But their love is hate.
   O Lord, how long ?

Their talk is of prayer ;
They rejoice in dim light and low music and the
  subtle beauties of the Prayer-Book ;
Tears come to their eyes and gentle tremors thrill
  their nerves ;
But their prayer is a dream.
   O Lord, how long ?

They bow down to the Christ ;
He is their dearly loved Lord and Master ;
They listen to His gospel and make it their
  task to see that it shall be preached to all
  nations ;
But He knows them not.
   O Lord, how long ?

A Psalm for the Poor

It was for us, His gospel;
He named it, " Good tidings to the poor ";
He gave it to us, their brothers, who cannot enter
      their homes, or else must eat at another table
      and steal up back-stairs to the garret.
He never spoke to us of the stations to which we
      are called ;
He called all men to one station—not to be ministered
      unto, but to minister ;
But their eyes, as they read, are holden.
        O Lord, how long ?

VI

When they despise us they despise themselves, for
      are we not one ?
When they separate themselves from us and measure
      their height from our baseness, do they not
      degrade themselves in us, and are they not
      traitors to our common humanity ?
A house divided against itself cannot stand.
Their high rank is high treason.
        O Lord, how long ?

VII

But lo, the Son of Man cometh !
Their best self bends down to each of them ;

A Psalm for the Poor

The age-spirit of love breathes within them;
The light of truth flashes forth once more as the
    lightning that cometh out of the east and
    shineth even unto the west;
Will it be rejected too of this generation?
      O Lord, how long?

VIII

O ye that begin to see and hear,
    Love now, live now.
The hour is coming and now is
When the dead shall hear the voice of the Son of
    God, and they that hear shall live.
Away with the barriers, then; clasp your brethren
    to your bosoms;
Let there be no hesitation, no compromise, no reser-
    vations, no misgivings.
Let him which is on the housetop not come down
    to take anything out of his house,
Neither let him which is in the field return back to
    take his clothes.
Have ye not talked long enough?
Will ye never live?
      O Lord, how long?

/ Now I understand ❧

I TAKE my place in the lower classes.
    I renounce the title of gentleman because it
    has become intolerable to me.
Dear Master, I understand now why you too took
    your place in the lower classes,
And why you refused to be a gentleman.

It's none of our Affair ❧

WE'VE loosed ourselves from Calvin's chain ;
    No bigots blind are we ;
The freedom of our heart and brain
    Is beautiful to see.

No more are infants doomed, we trust,
    To burn in hottest hell ;
For such a fate would be unjust,
    As anyone might tell.

Of course they are condemned on earth
    To pine in wretched slums,
But then, they'll have no end of mirth
    When heaven's kingdom comes.

It's none of our Affair

And if meanwhile they die like flies
    From lack of food and air,
As you may readily surmise,
    It's none of our affair.

The dogma of election, too,
    Is more absurd than this ;
God for no arbitrary few
    Reserves eternal bliss.

Of course, a few of us on earth
    Inherit all the plums,
But we shall lose our rights of birth
    When heaven's kingdom comes.

And if meanwhile it is our fate
    To feast on choicest fare,
While men lie begging at our gate,
    It's none of our affair.

Again, we hardly are content,
    That for the things we've done
Our Judge should wreak His punishment
    Upon a guiltless one.

Of course our toilers bear on earth
    Their cross, till each succumbs ;
'Tis time enough to crown their worth
    When heaven's kingdom comes.

And if meanwhile luxurious ease,
And vice and want of care,
Make us exploit the lives of these,
It's none of our affair.

And so, you see, in heaven above,
Where we have never been,
We've stablished justice, peace, and love,
And put an end to sin.

And all religious bigotry
We've swept from heart and mind.
Of course from cant we're also free,
Of economic kind.

For if meanwhile a hell on earth
Is spreading everywhere,
And plenty roots itself in dearth,
It's none of our affair.

The Dead Sin

I

I SEE the Master eating with publicans and sinners,
refusing to condemn the adulteress, opening
paradise to the thief;

40

The Dead Sin

Showing His love in His eyes as He speaks long-
    ingly to the young man, notwithstanding the
    youth's enslavement to riches, his refusal of
    freedom ;
Himself numbered among the transgressors, whose
    friendship He sought ;
And yet indignant, with words which still reverberate
    down the centuries, against hypocrites and
    against them only,
Singling out one sin from all sins for utter reproba-
    tion.

II

Hypocrisy, thou art indeed a sin apart, a sin of
    death amid sins of life, a dead disease amid
    living diseases,
A stiffening of joints, a hardening of tissues, ossify-
    ing man into a lifeless form, binding him to
    the dead forms of the past, shutting him out
    for ever from the life that is to be ;
While ye, ye sins of passion and ambition, are at
    least alive ;
Though your life be that of the disease-germ and
    tumour, it is still life ;
Its teeming energy may be reclaimed ; it may be
    turned into new channels ;
And who can foresee the fruitage it may yet bring
    forth ?

The Dead Sin

Inertia, death, these alone are surely fatal to life.
He who came that men might have life and have
    it more abundantly—
What truce could there be between Him and death?

III

Ye other sins, like covetousness, ye are idolatry,
But have ye not at least your idols set up before
    you? do ye not at least worship something?
Your face is turned to the future; you climb the
    steps of some temple, though it be the wrong
    temple;
Ye have a motive, and really act and live; for you
    there is still hope.
But hypocrisy is a mere simulacrum; it has the
    name to live and is dead:
It has no God, no idol, no ideal;
Its stony stare is riveted on the past;
It cannot grow and develop; it is doomed to eternal
    arrest and stagnation;
It is the sin of death, and for it is the woe of
    despair.
He who came that men might have life and have it
    more abundantly—
What truce could there be between Him and death?

Hypocrites and Hypocrites ❧

ARE we not a little too free with this tempting
word, " hypocrite " ?

We Single Taxers, who denounce landlords, and yet
pocket gladly the unearned ground-rent ourselves ;

We socialist lecturers, who say, " Competition is of
the devil, but so long as you permit it we
shall continue to profit by it " ;

We anarchists, who go on judging and condemning,
and suing and being sued ;

We, all of us, who wait for society to make the first
step, and are not perhaps after all in such
great haste that it should take us at our
word ?

How do we differ from the abolitionist slave-holder,
or the drunken temperance preacher, or any
other moral monster ?

Who are we, to throw stones at our brother hypocrites
of respectability ?

Nay, we cannot shoulder our sins upon society ;

Rather should we take upon ourselves the sins of
others,

Make for them and for us the supreme effort to do
right as well as to talk right ; ,

43

/ And if we fail, at least fall fighting, struggling to
undo the bonds that bind us all. /

Folly, perhaps, but the folly that we must learn from
all the prophets, heroes, saints, and martyrs
of old ;

And if we learn it not, who are we to cast stones at
our brother hypocrites of respectability ?

Debit and Credit ❧

I

HALF the world is labouring to-day for you :
The Chinese coolie is hard at work pluck-
ing tea - leaves or wading in the rice - fields
for you ;

The Southern negro, the fellah of the Nile are sow-
ing cotton under a blazing sun for you ;

Factory men and women, and young girls and little
children, at home and abroad, are leading
cheerless, steam-driven lives for you ;

Farm labourers on the prairie are toiling with
sweating brows from sunrise to sunset for
you ;

You have slaves in every clime to-day, suffering
every degree of weariness and degradation—
and all for you.

What are you doing for them ?

Debit and Credit

Believe me, you cannot discharge this great obligation with money;

The recording angel, who keeps the book of life, knows no money except that which you have rightfully earned, and which is therefore your labour.

With other money you can only shift your duties upon the shoulders of others;

And these others already have their own duties, which they must neglect if they assume yours.

You must acquit yourself with your labour, and with your labour alone.

How, then, do your books stand?

Is the balance hopelessly against you?

If so, acknowledge your bankruptcy; tell yourself no lies; begin life again.

Henceforth insist on giving more than you get, and on serving rather than being served;

Even as the Son of Man came not to be ministered unto but to minister.

The Shipwreck

I

THE coast of a desert island in the Southern
Sea;
The cocoa-nut palms crowd down to the very beach,
where the waves still break angrily after the
tempest;
But overhead the sun is sinking in a clear sky, and
the pure, still air is laden with spices.
A company of shipwrecked men are busily engaged
at the edge of the grove:
Some are gathering cocoa-nuts; some are cutting
them in two to make cups and to get at the
rich kernel;
Others are bringing wood and kindling a fire to dry
their clothes and cook their supper;
Still others are building rude shelters and wind-
brakes of boughs, and heaping up beds of
leaves.

II

It is a strange, unnatural sight to our civilised eyes,
for not one is idle.
First cabin and steerage have been forgotten for
once.

46

The Shipwreck

The man of wealth elbows the poor emigrant and the deck-hand, and his hands are as grimy as theirs.

His purse is in his pocket, but he does not take it out and cry, " Here is gold ; labour for me."

Such a thought never occurs to him, and if it did he knows that they would scoff at his yellow toys.

The clergyman is hard at work. He does not say, " Cook my dinner and let me sit still ; I will preach to you on Sunday."

The judge and the lawyer are sweating like day-labourers ; neither of them says, " We will decide your disputes when you fall to quarrelling, and will punish you when we are of opinion that you have committed crimes ; meanwhile, build the best huts and make the best beds for us, even if you, who do the work, have to sleep on the bare ground and under the open heavens."

They have been saying these things all their lives. How is it that they have suddenly ceased to say them ?

Ah, the storm has cleared the air !

It has swept the dark clouds of economics and lies far below the horizon.

For the first time our travellers are face to face with nature, and behold at last their natural duties ;

The Shipwreck

They have unconsciously made the discovery that
they are men, and neither more nor less than
men ;
Here they must be as simple and direct and true as
the palm trees over their heads or the pebbles
beneath their feet.

III

Alas, it may be for only a few weeks at most !
Even if they remain here, ere long the old serpent
with his three heads—rent, interest, and profit
—will tempt them again to eat the forbidden
fruit of others' labour.
Would there not soon be another fall, another dis-
graceful eviction from paradise, the angel
sentinel again on guard at the entrance to
their better natures ?

IV

My brothers, we too are cast up together for a time
by the sea of eternity on this remote, mysterious island-globe of ours.
What privilege can any one of us claim ?
Shall we not do our share of the rough-and-tumble
work ?
Can we without shame lie dreaming or chatting or
scribbling under the palms while the rest are
toiling ?

And if we have seized for ourselves the monopoly of
　　thinking,
Should we not at least think straight and see
　　straight?
Verily, we of all others should have thought out the
　　truth of the old law of nature, " He that will
　　not work, neither shall he eat."

The New Envoys ❧

I

SEE the chasm between rich and poor ever
　　widening,
The newly invented millionaire and tramp marking
　　the greatest stretch;
More charities, but less fellow-feeling; more patron-
　　age, but less sympathy.
If disdain hardly cares to hide itself on one side, can
　　we wonder if we detect hate and envy on the
　　other?
And yet even envy and hatred may be in part
　　purified by a sense of injustice, of righteous
　　indignation, of a common cause.
What God hath joined, man is putting asunder.
We are cutting an ugly gash in the flesh of
　　humanity, and are slowly waking to the
　　naked shame.

The New Envoys

But how bravely and tenderly nature seeks to heal
    the ghastliest wound,
Tissue striving to knit itself to tissue,
Muscle, sinew, flesh doing their best to bridge the
    abyss,
Groping outward tentatively, longing to meet a like
    growth from the other side, and once more to
    help mould all together in the old union.
And so with us, behold the first envoys of recon-
    ciliation,
Young men and women leaving ease and comfort
    and idleness to live in the slums of our great
    cities ;
Sacrificing self, because they cannot do otherwise ;
Yet living gladly, finding new, undreamt-of joys in
    life.
See in far Russia one nobleman after another donning
    the peasant's sheepskin, working in the fields,
    going to the people ;
And so in Prussia, the rich land-owner marrying a
    peasant woman, sending his children to the
    village school, delighting in a new - found
    sense of brotherhood ;
In Belgium, the young baron insisting on sitting in
    the patrician senate in a labourer's blouse,
    proud only of his manhood ;

In England, the university don throwing up his
fellowship, choosing to share a workman's
cottage, tilling a market - garden, preaching
simplicity and fraternity, writing books that
will live.

III

" Fools," says the world, " harbouring a false senti-
ment, and then overdoing it ;
Degenerates, mattoids, cranks, at least unbalanced ! "
Nay, rather strong types and symbols of the fellowship to be ;
Taking upon themselves the sins of their age ;
Leaping into the chasm that it may close behind them.
Overdoing perhaps, but what a glorious overdoing it
is ! how necessary as a graphic protest against
the wrongs that be, how well designed to
arrest the mind of the drowsy world and
shake it from its mediæval dreams.
I love them all, with their sheepskins and blouses,
and peasant wives and children—
Love them as the heralds of the coming time, as the
vigorous, homely, accentuated words of destiny.
Such were the prophets of old,
Preaching the word of the Lord in their deeds,
Fitting the symbol to the lesson as they walked the
streets,
Living epistles, read of all men.

Nay, such was the Master Himself, who for our sakes
   became poor, that we through His poverty
   might become rich.

The Wealth of St. Francis ❧

The Wealth of St. Francis

I

I T is noontide on the public square of Assisi ;
   The black shadows are at their shortest on
   the glaring white pavement.
A crowd comes up the street.
Bernardone, the rich father of Francis, seeks the
   Bishop, to complain of his son, who is wasting
   all his substance in almsgiving.
Francis, a mere lad, follows with them, and the
   children are throwing stones at him, while
   their parents point him out with derision.
The Bishop descends the steps of his palace with
   his attendants.
The youth hastens to meet him, and suddenly strips
   off his fine raiment and casts it at his father's
   feet.
The old man strives to strike him, but his friends
   hold him back.
IIis son sees him not, however ; he is looking all
   absorbed toward the sky.

The Wealth of St. Francis

"Henceforth," he cries, "I have only a Father in heaven; I renounce all earthly possessions; I confide my treasure to Him, and He will provide."

The kindly Bishop, with tears in his eyes, covers the naked youth with his mantle, and his followers receive him among themselves.

Many in the crowd gaze scornfully at the young saint, as if he were a lunatic; others show pity in their faces; a few seem to be impressed by his faith, but not one is prophet enough to understand the effect of that strange scene upon the history of the world.

II

Years have passed.

The friars of St. Francis have preached to the common people a new religion—the religion of conscious love to God and of fellowship to man, of self-respect and freedom for the individual, and of contempt for riches.

They radiate a wonderful force, which they derive from their founder.

He took all that lived and moved to his bosom, and thence drew his strength.

The birds and flowers, the wolf and the ass, the sun and moon, were his brothers and sisters.

The Wealth of St. Francis

He brought Christ down from heaven, and God with
 Him.

Jesus walked the earth again; His disciples again
 hung on His arm; once more they watched
 His loving, mysterious face.

Human love was no longer impious, but became a
 reflection of the Divine love.

Francis taught his little brothers, and they taught
 the masses to feel, in part at least, as he
 himself did.

He aroused a new enthusiasm for mankind, and a
 new sympathy for earth and sea and sky.

This is the seed which he and his band scattered,
 and the harvest springs up in glorious Christian
 art.

III

A great church grows at Assisi over the beloved
 body of the saint, and from it shoots forth
 the new Gothic architecture of Italy.

On its walls Giotto revels in the life of his hero, and
 his frescoes mark a new day in the history of
 man.

The inspiration of Francis calls to life a natural and
 dramatic art beneath the artist's hands.

Giotto becomes, too, the greatest architect of all time,
 and builds the Campanile at Florence out of
 his heavenly dreams.

The Wealth of St. Francis

Moved by the same spirit, Niccolo Pisano and his successors revive the ancient art of sculpture and make the marble warm with life.

The impulse is given which in due time will lead to Raphael, and Titian, and Michael Angelo, and the rest.

Francis, too, begins to sing hymns in the language of the people.

He is himself a poet, and among his disciples also are poets ;

They produce the " Dies Irae," and the " Stabat Mater," and many a popular song in the vulgar tongue ;

Until at last the stream of poetry widens into the boundless sea of Dante.

And so of Francis of Assisi is born the poetry, the sculpture, the painting, the architecture of Christendom.

He may indeed claim as his offspring the new-born marvel of Christian art.

What miracle is this ?

The man who flung all possessions from him endows mankind with its noblest wealth ;

He who threw away gold and silver in exchange for truth and love proves after all to be the wisest economist ;

His folly outstrips all the wisdom of the world !

Politics 🐛

I

THE great, living, growing, changing world of
    public opinion,—
How it overshadows the little political world of
    manufactured law !
In the former we are all legislators by our birthright ;
We owe to it the frankest, most honest expression of
    our views ;
For its sake we must for ever insist on the fullest
    freedom of speech for ourselves and others.
All the mighty men of all time have been leaders
    in this parliament ;
We rejoice in maintaining its high traditions.

II

For a maker of public opinion, an hereditary man,
    what attraction can politics have ?
Its dream of influence is an illusion,
For they leave their real selves behind who enter
    there ;
Their new influence is that of their false selves.
They no longer dare to say what they believe ;
They must strive to think what they think that
    others think that they ought to think ;

They must resign their seat in the parliament of the
    world;
To rule, they must deliver themselves up, bound hand
    and foot, to others;
To extend their sway they must become slaves.
/ The political world is a government by slaves in
    quest of slaves.
If we enter it, we sell our birthright for a mess of
    pottage. ✓

✓ Go on ❦

GO on with your voting and organising,
    Your judging and condemning and punish-
ing,
Your recruiting and drilling and building of war-
    ships.
You say it is your duty.
I think that perhaps it is.
All I know is that it is not mine, and that some
    day it will cease to be yours.
The time will come when you will have grown
    beyond all that,
When you will see the absurdity of it all,
When you will lay aside childish things.
Go on then; play with your bats and balls and tops
    and pocket-knives;

The New Freedom

Bump your heads; stub your toes; cut your fingers
and let them bleed; learn from your only
schoolmistress—Pain.

You cannot share our experiences; you must each
have your own.

When you have at last finished your term, and left
the narrow school and playground,

We will give you a rousing welcome in the real
world outside,

Where men live one degree nearer the cause of things,

And where the air is clearer and the sunlight
brighter. ╱

The New Freedom ☙

I

AMERICANS, you once were free,—
Free as the broad prairie and the forest
profound,—

And then, after your Revolution, you led the world.

Your example fired France, and France set Europe
aflame.

Without battalions or men of war you were in the
van of the nations.

A mere handful, living in straggling hamlets along
a thousand miles of narrow seaboard;

The New Freedom

Without arms, you were invincible;
Without a fortress, you were invulnerable.
Your strength was your freedom.

II

Times change, and freedom changes with them,
For freedom must from age to age be born again.
The political liberty of Seventy-six, the equality
    before the law, of which you talk so much,
    is no longer the living ideal that it was;
It is now a fossil for antiquaries to toy with.
Will you play with it in the rear while the nations
    go marching on?

III

Think you to lead again by dint of armies and
    navies and coast defences?
Not so is the world mastered.
Spread your frontiers, take Cuba and Hawaii, beguile
    Canada if you can, push on over the great
    Southern Hemisphere;
Will these lands be yours?
There is only one possession in them worth the
    capturing, and that is the hearts of men;
And these hearts can never be won by a nation of
    slaves.
Be free, and all mankind will flock to your standard.

The New Freedom

IV

While you talk of freedom, do you not feel the
fetters that are fastening on your limbs?
While you hurrah, are you unconscious of the burden
which you are bearing?
Are you never weary of the endless task?
Can you still be cheered by the devilish dream of
becoming taskmasters in your turn?
Up, and to death with the tyrant!
Let there be no half measures; he must be torn from
his insolent throne.
Show him no quarter; plunge the dagger in deep
and again and again; let him welter in his
blood.

There, at last you are rising.   Where is the
oppressor, do you cry?
You will not find him in the streets.
Look for him in your own souls, for the kingdom of
hell is within you.
There reigns the greed for gold;
There it is that you are either trampling on your
fellow-men or longing to be numbered with
the tramplers;
There it is that your rebellion, your revolution must
begin.

Set yourselves free. Away with the usurper; enthrone
in his stead the new ideal, the equal freedom
in love of all mankind, liberty and union, one
and inseparable.

Ah yes; seek first the kingdom of heaven, and all
things shall be added unto you.

Prophets ❧

I

HAPPY the land that knoweth its prophets
before they die!

Happy the land that doth not revile and persecute
them during their lives!

Was there ever such a land?

We are still engaged in the ancient pastime—

Building the monuments of the prophets of old,

And casting stones at the seers whom we meet in
the streets.

In the world's market one dead prophet is worth a
dozen of the living.

Happy the land that knoweth its prophets before
they die!

II

We, Pharisees of the Jerusalem of Herod,

We do reverence indeed to the words of Isaiah and
Amos.

Prophets

Did they pitch into rulers and landlords rather
roughly?

Why, in those distant times, landlords and rulers
richly deserved it.

If we had been in the days of our fathers, we would
not have been partakers with them in the
blood of the prophets.

But what shall we do with this man, Jesus, who talks
in much the same strain?

Oh, away with Him! Crucify Him! crucify Him!

Happy the land that knoweth its prophets before
they die!

III

And still we rehearse the same dismal comedy, even
in America, and in this Nineteenth Century.

How did we hail John Brown, and Thoreau, and
Whitman?

Behold Garrison! The astounding, intrepid youth
advances single-handed with his sling against
the ogre of slavery.

One day he is mobbed and almost massacred on the
streets of Boston, under the shadow of the
statues of Franklin and Washington, because
he preaches freedom.

Now at last his monument too stands, honoured by
all, at the heart of the Puritan city.

How fare the living prophets in Boston to-day?

Happy the land that knoweth its prophets before
    they die !

IV

And there are prophets to-day, though the world
    passes them by unheeding.
Their race is not extinct, and will not be until we
    settle down to death.
To them is confided the life of the world.
On the bold, startling lines they lay down, the
    living structure of the future will grow;
The nerve-like shapes which they trace in the
    amorphous and distorted mass of society will
    by and by be centres of visible life, and take
    on flesh and blood.
Believe me, these partners in creation live; I have
    seen them—the apostles of manhood, of justice,
    of simplicity.
They can afford to wait.
If they received now their deserved acclaim we
    might well doubt their right to rank with the
    prophets.
Our children will build the monuments of Tolstoy,
    and George, and the rest;
But how will they treat their own prophets?
Happy the land that knoweth its prophets before
    they die !

√ **Revolt** ❧

I

HAIL, spirit of revolt, thou spirit of life,
   Child of the ideal, daughter of the far-away
   truth!
Without thee the nations drag on in a living death;
Without thee is stagnation and arrested growth;
Without thee Europe and America would be sunk in
      China's lethargy,
Smothered in the past, having no horizon but the
      actual.

II

Hail, spirit of revolt, thou spirit of life,
Child of eternal love,—
Love rebelling against lovelessness, life rebelling
      against death!
Rise at last to the full measure of thy birthright;
Spurn the puny weapons of hate and oppression;
Fix rather thy calm, burning, protesting eyes on all
      the myriad shams of man, and they will fade
      away in thinnest air;
Gaze upon thy gainsayers until they see and feel the
      truth and love that begat and bore thee.
Thus and thus only give form and body to thy
      noblest aspirations,

64

And we shall see done on earth as it is in heaven
God's ever living, growing, ripening will. ✓

The Prison ༅

AND I saw a gaol lifting its grimy walls to
heaven.

And they that passed by looked at it askance, for
they said, " It is the abode of Sin."

And to them the broad sky and all the earth was
fair to look upon, for they saw the early buds
opening and heard the birds that had come
back from the South, and they felt the sun
which was new warming the hearts of beast
and plant.

But within the prison, and behind its cold, thick
buttresses, and its small, round, triple-barred
windows, that looked like tunnels, they heard
faint groanings and sighings and much lamentation, and they said, " It is most just, for it
is the abode of Sin."

And I heard a Voice saying, "Woe to the cause
that hath not passed through a prison ! "

And I looked again, and I saw in the gaol those
deliverers who in each age have saved the
world from itself and set it free, and gyves
were on their wrists and ankles.

5 65

The Prison

And I saw Israel in the house of bondage before it
came forth to preserve Duty for mankind.

Woe to the cause that hath not passed through a
prison!

And I saw the Prætorian Hall and One that was
bound therein, and the soldiers bowed the
knee before Him and mocked Him and then
led Him away to proclaim Love to the
world.

Woe to the cause that hath not passed through a
prison!

And I saw within the gaol them that gave liberty to
the slave, and them that unbound the mind of
man, and them that strove to free his conscience, and them that led onward to Freedom
and Justice and Love.

Woe to the cause that hath not passed through a
prison!

And I saw there also those who in our own time
have counted themselves as nothing if they
could but point out God's way unto their
brethren; and there were many, too, of the
prophets who are still to come, and these also
were in bonds.

Woe to the cause that hath not passed through a
prison!

And lo, the sky became clouded, and night fell, and
there were no birds nor blossoms, but a chill

came upon the earth, and they that passed by shivered and trembled; and I beheld, and saw that they were not men, but that they were really wolves, and apes, and swine.

And within the gaol was a great light, and a pleasant warmth came from the barred windows, and I heard a burst of triumphant song.

And the gyves fell from the limbs of the prisoners, and there was great joy.

And they that passed by would now come in but they could not; and now within was freedom and without was captivity.

And the hosts within held up their arms, and the marks of their shackles were upon them.

But I hid my hands behind me, for there was no mark on my wrists.

Woe to the cause that hath not passed through a prison!

The State-House ❧

U P to the State-House wend their way
    Some scores of thieves elect;
For one great recompense they pray:
" May we grow rich from day to day,
    Although the State be wrecked."

The State-House

Up to the State-House climbs with stealth
   Another pilgrim band,—
The thieves who have acquired their wealth,
And, careless of their country's health,
   Now bleed their native land.

And soon the yearly sale is made
   Of privilege and law;
The poor thieves by the rich are paid
Across the counter, and a trade
   More brisk you never saw.

And we, whose rights are bought and sold,
   With reason curse and swear;
Such acts are frightful to behold,
Nor has the truth been ever told
   Of half the evil there.

At last the worthless set adjourn;
   We sigh with deep relief.
Then from the statute-book we learn
The record of each theft in turn,
   The bills of every thief.

Now at a shameful scene pray look;
   For we who cursed and swore,
Before this base-born statute-book,
Whose poisoned source we ne'er mistook,
   Both worship and adore.

" For law is law," we loud assert,
   And think ourselves astute ;
Yet quite forgetful, to our hurt,
That fraud is fraud and dirt is dirt,
   And like must be their fruit.

We laugh at heathen who revere
   The gods they make of stone,
And yet we never ask, I fear,
As we bow down from year to year,
   How we have made our own.

We all deny the right of kings
   To speak for their Creator ;
May we not wonder, then, whence springs
The right divine to order things
   Of any legislator ?

Divus Augustus

HEARKEN to the chorus of the overfed.
   Their eyes stand out with fatness ; they
have more than heart could wish, and their
raiment is purple and fine linen.
Listen to them as they sing :—

Divus Augustus

" All hail to thee, Authority!   Hail to thy ministers;
    hail ye powers that be, kings and presidents,
    judges and makers of laws!
Hail to thee, Authority!
Thou standest in high places, and stablishest the
    earth.
Thou bringest the wicked low, and appointest his
    reward to the upright.
Thou preservest our goods unto us, and prosperest
    the work of our hands.
But upon him who would oppose our righteous ways
    thou layest thy heavy hand;
Thou leadest him unto bondage, and he is brought in
    sorrow to the grave.
Thou causest peace to reign upon the earth, for thou
    separatest the troublers from the congregation
    of the just.
Thou makest the nations rich in glory and honour.
All hail to thee, Authority!"

Now the chorus retires and another advances.
This is the hungry chorus; we can count their bones
    through their rags.
Hearken to them as they sing :—

" Woe to thee, O Authority, O Moloch!
Thou forbiddest murder, and art the prince of
    murderers,—

Teaching the sons of men how best to slay their
    brethren ;

Building mighty engines to fill the world with blood
    and every kind of horror ;

Shaping great ships, that they may send other
    ships with all on board to the bottom of
    the sea.

Thou condemnest and takest life, though thy judges
    be baser than their prisoners.

Thou settest up him with a beam in his eye to take
    out the mote from his brother's.

Thou ordainest him that hath sinned to cast the
    first stone.

" Thou forbiddest robbery, and art the prince of
    robbers,—

Thou takest the earth, God's gift to men, from the
    many and givest it to the few, and thus thou
    makest the poor to pay for his own ;

There is no spot where he can labour or lie down
    and rest, or where his wife can bring forth
    her first-born, or where he can bury his dead,
    without offering tribute of his hard-earned
    wage to thy creatures.

Thou takest the fruit of his toil, and dividest it to
    the idle.

Thou makest him to work many hours, that the rich
    may live without labour.

Divus Augustus

The toiler hath no time to learn and to attain to the
full measure of a man.

He can but work, eat, and sleep, so that the privileged
may be surfeited with knowledge and pleasure.

And thus thou stealest his brains for them that
already have his wealth in their houses.

" Woe unto thy ministers, O Authority!

Woe unto you, ye powers that be, kings and presidents, judges and makers of laws!

Your ways are full of craftiness, of bribery, and
intrigue, and betrayal of friends ;

Of pride, haughtiness, craving, and disappointment,
and hardness of heart ;

Of contempt for all that is humble, useful, and worthy ;

Of hatred, malice, and all uncharitableness ;

Of cringing, envy, and compromise with evil ;

Of ambition, selfishness, bitterness, and corruption.

In the wild struggle for life, the violent seize the reins.

Ye are made drunk with power, until ye think yourselves a race apart.

Ye pretend to all the virtues and honours, and are
the high priests of hypocrisy.

" Woe to thee, Authority!

Thy crimes are not like the common felon's, which
all abhor, and thence learn a lesson of righteousness.

But thou crownest thy sins with glory;
Thou deckest them with silver and gold, and callest
upon all to bow the knee.
Freedom is often upon thy lips, but thy foot hath
alway rested on the neck of the slave.
Thou hast imprisoned and murdered the prophets of
old,
And now thou buildest their monuments and perse-
cutest them of to-day;
Wherefore thou art a witness unto thyself that thou
art the same Authority which killedst the
prophets.
Thou sayest Peace, peace, when there is no peace.
Can there be peace, when from the least of thy
minions even unto the greatest of them everyone is given to covetousness?
What hath peace to do where violence and spoil are
become the pillars of the commonwealth?
Woe unto thee, Authority!"

The song has ended.
Who shall decide the issue?

.   .   .   .   .

To the Russian People &

I

W E look behind your mask, O People of Russia;
 We penetrate beyond the shameless, domi-
 neering, robbing, famine - breeding Government; beyond the thin veneer of borrowed
 culture and vice.

We gaze into your eyes until we behold your heart
 there.

We see the long-suffering, patient endurance with
 which you carry your heavy load;

Your uncomplaining faith in your destiny as men,

Your loving-kindness for your fellows, your natural
 affinity for the Christ-life.

We see these, in spite of all your faults, and in those
 faults themselves we recognise the fruit of im-
 memorial oppression.

II

Our hearts go out to you, O Russian People;

Your vast land is big with fate for the world.

We look for no barbarian invasion from the old
 fountain of nations in the East;

We expect no continued stretching and stiffening of
 the bonds of your empire;

74

On the Rejection of the Treaty of 1897

But we hail the new dawn there of the old familiar
 good tidings to the poor, rising again upon
 another and brighter day.
We look to you confidently for a new proclamation
 of the message of peace, goodwill towards
 men.

On the Rejection of the General Arbitration Treaty of 1897

SHAME on a Senate which withstands
 The efforts of two mighty lands
Frankly to grasp each other's hands!

Are they our servants?   Should they then
Bring all our dreams to nought again
Of peace on earth, goodwill toward men?

From every class—North, South, East, West—
Goes up one earnest, loud request,
" Give us our treaty, and be blest!"

The working man, with outstretched hand
Asks but to work, makes one demand—
That peace and plenty cheer the land.

On the Rejection of the Treaty of 1897

But no ; this deaf, degenerate crew
Want plenty solely for the few.
Let war then split our race in two.

Turn back the years ; let growth stand still,
And flourish every social ill,
If so these triflers get their fill.

Let bluster, envy, spite, conceit,
Elate at this, their latest feat,
Boast that their victory is complete.

What monarch, drunk with martial lust,
Treading his subjects in the dust,
E'er proved more recreant to his trust?

Are these our patriots, these, the blind,
Whose love of country is combined
With petty hate for all mankind?

Nay, from their rule we pray release ;
Soon may such love of country cease.
They know not love that love not peace.

The Nation's Life

I

L OOK not in the senate halls for the life of the
nation.
Their talk is the talk of dreamers;
They reel as drunken men;
They grope like the blind in the dark.
The form of life is there, but the spirit hath long
since fled.

II

Look not chiefly in the church or the press;
There indeed are dim glimmerings,
Faint hints of a possible revival,
Half-stifled cries that tell of discontent and pain;
And where there is pain, there is life.
But, alas, these signs are so few!

III

Look rather among the discredited and outcast.
Meet with them in dingy upper rooms.
Find, under all their extravagance and error, the
sound-ringing ore of hope.
The stone which the builders reject will again be-
come the head of the corner;
For this is the universal law of life.

77

A Chorus for the European

Wherever two or three are gathered in love and self-
forgetfulness, to make the world better;
Wherever men think and feel profoundly, and then
go forth to act accordingly—
Look there for the nation's life.

A Chorus for the European
"Concert" of 1897 ᴥ

I

LET the Armenians be imprisoned and die.
What care we for massacres? What matters
it if a few thousands perish, so taxes be levied
and interest comes in on the very day fixed
in the bond?

A man with a bond in his pocket is worth five
hundred with bonds on their arms and legs.

Long live the Turk, for he owes us money.

There is no Armenian debt,—so much the worse for
the Armenians,—or we might think it worth
while to protect them.

Who says that a national debt is not a national
blessing?

Long live property and the golden bond which
unites men and nations—the bond of debtor
and creditor.

78

But we must interfere to help the poor oppressed
    Turk in Crete, for his name is on our bonds.
Down with the wretched Cretans!
They do not owe us anything;
Why, then, should they cumber the ground?
Oh, all ye nations of the world, if ye wish to live in
    safety and happiness,
Come to our pawnshops, and borrow and borrow,
    and bind yourselves soul and body to us.
Long live property and national debts, and bonds,
    bonds, bonds!
May no Moses ever arise to lead the people out of
    this house of bondage.
Did anyone say "Liberty"? Nay, put him out;
    drown the discord.
Long live property, property, property!

The Election of 1896

THE honest dollar!
    A good motto that to catch the unwary,
But misapplied to any idol, gold or silver;
A watchword destined, perhaps, some day to adorn
    another standard,
When men have at last delved down to the deeper
    issue.

The Narrow Path

The honest dollar—
The dollar earned by useful, glad, equivalent,
    honoured labour,
Pitted against the shame-faced dollar—
The dollar begged, borrowed, extorted, or stolen.

The Narrow Path ❧

WE are still sitting by the wayside.
    We heard the old cry, "Come out of her,
My people," and we determined to escape
from the wickedness of the world.
We forsook all, and turned into the steep, narrow
    path that seemed to lead out.
We had not climbed long before we met another
    band returning, ragged, emaciated, and foot-
    sore.
"Turn back," they whispered hoarsely. "We too
    heard the cry, and we have pushed on to the
    end of the path.
"Oh, the bitter, hard, monotonous, weary journey!
"And there at the end we saw a gate, and an angel
    standing with a flaming sword which turned
    every way, to keep the way of paradise.
"And the angel said, 'Who are ye?'
"And we answered, 'We be men who would escape
    the sin of the world.'

"And he said, 'Where are all your brethren ? Are
ye not their keepers ? '

"And we replied, 'We have left them behind us.'

"But the angel frowned and shook his head.

"'How can ye hope to come forth alone ? ' he
cried.

"'Did not God give you a world stored with all good
things, enough and to spare ?

"'Have ye not so used them that want and hunger
and vice stalk about among you ?

"'While in the market-place starving men stand all
the day idle, others of you know not what to
do with their surfeit.

"'Every man worketh in the fear that to-morrow he
may no longer find work to do.

"'Ye have brought things to such a pass that the
evil-doer is your greatest benefactor.

"'He that wasteth his substance in riotous living, he
that destroyeth the wealth ye have made, he
that setteth fire to a city, is even a blessing
to the land, for he giveth work to them that
need it.

"'He that maketh away with his fellow, the wanton
slayer of his brother, is a public benefactor ; for
he either removeth him that could find no work,
and was hence a burden upon you, or else he
maketh room among the workers for one of
the idle.

6 81

The Narrow Path

" ' And so your wise men pray for war as a god-send, and shut out the men and the wealth of other countries at your ports ; and in thus doing evil they bless your land.

" ' And he that doeth good among you is become your torment.

" ' Everyone who turneth to useful work maketh others idle and taketh the bread from the mouths of their children.

" ' Every artificer in brass and iron who inventeth an engine by which one man may easily do the toil of an hundred, and which should thus give rest and leisure and plenty to thousands,

" ' Every such an one becometh a curse to thousands, for he taketh away their means of livelihood.

" ' And while thus your men stand useless and helpless,

" ' Ye lay your burdens on your women and little children ;

" ' And they fill your factories and workshops from the rising of the sun even unto the going down of the same.

" ' And this is what ye have done with the talents which were given you.

" ' Your trade is builded upon oppression, and lying, and fraud, and adulteration ;

" ' Ye have so limited the bounty of God that the fear of failure doggeth every man's steps, and he

seeketh safety in a rivalry that would shame
the devils in hell.

"'Your one motto is ever, "Outstrip your neighbour; either he goes under, or you."

"'And ye would escape alone from this world that
ye have made?

"'Ye who have needs done wrong every day and
hour,

"'Ye who have made good evil and evil good,

"'Ye who are part and parcel of your bankrupt race,

"'Would ye now hide your talent in a napkin?

"'Would ye flee from the rest, and leave them to go
on sinning for you and in your stead?

"'Nay, not so. Go back and suffer altogether.

"'Proclaim a fast, and put on sackcloth, from the
greatest of you even unto the least of you.

"'In your humiliation not one of you must be left
out. Ye can only escape from sin by taking
their sin upon you and leading them all out
of sin.

"'Go back and make your own paradise, for ye
would sicken and die here in a separate
heaven of your own.'

"And the angel ceased. And we turned and fled, for
we saw that there was no issue to this path.
Come back with us; come back."

And the little band passed on down the steep,
winding path,

Doubt

While we sat down at the wayside and looked at
  each other, and wondered whether they had
  heard the angel aright. ✓

Doubt ❧

I

THE work of the world is bound up with injustice and oppression ;
I cannot even hoe potatoes without cheapening them
  and throwing men out of employment.
Must I then renounce my part in the daily task of the
  human race so that I may remain blameless ?
Ah, blamelessness is a poor, negative goal, even if it
  were possible to reach it.
Must I hide my talent in a napkin lest it be soiled ?

II

The great captains of industry, with all their sins,
  still carry on the business of mankind ;
May I not lend a hand, for fear of sharing in fraud
  and extortion ?
Does my conscience point that way ?
And what if my conscience grows stronger and more
  imperious,
Until it leaves no foothold for me in this world of
  wrong ?

III

Away, tempter! I cannot throw conscience over-
board.
It is my compass, and shows me my course. Further
than that I am ignorant.
I have no chart of heaven and earth, and I cannot
tell whither I am sailing;
But even in the darkness of the storm, when neither
land nor constellation is in view,
I can keep my eye on the needle and my hands on
the helm,
And steer straight.

IV

True, this course may lead to death. But what
then?
In such deaths life has ever found fresh impulse.
The proof that, as things are, man cannot live and
be honest—
Could anything rouse the world to better things
more surely than such proof?
Witnesses to this fact, though they die in testifying,
martyrs though they become, these too have
their share, their blameless share, in bearing
the world onward on their shoulders.

A Walk in the Woods ❧

I

I WALK alone in the June forest.
   The great leaves of the oak seedlings hide
the ground between the tree-trunks.
A startled chipmunk runs across my path.
A black-poll warbler, perched on a hemlock bough
   close by me, cries " screep-screep " to his mate,
   and pays no attention to me.
Here, four centuries ago, before ever the pale-face
   peered in among the hickory and chestnut
   trees, the Indian chief was wont to stride,
   proud in his paint and feathers.
Come back, my red-skinned brother; give me your
   hand, and let us thread our way together
   through the familiar woods.
You cannot understand me; I can only guess at
   you; but still I see that in some things you
   are my superior.
I admire your simple life, your carelessness of
   hoarded wealth,
The equality of your customs, producing neither
   paupers nor millionaires.
I appreciate your stalwart frame, your piercing eye
   and sensitive ear, your exultant courage in
   battle, your unflinching submission to torture;

A Walk in the Woods

But above all I am fain to covet your unhesitating
acceptance of your lot.
You are on such friendly terms with the great
Mystery!
You do not pester it, as I do, with unseemly
questions;
You are not beset with a sickly inquisitiveness;
You take your proper place in the Mystery itself, as
the swallow makes his nest in the barn, and
you trouble it as little as it troubles you.

II

And yet I know that I am farther advanced than
you are.
This journey from you to me had to be travelled;
These questions had to be put; the answers had to
be wearily sought.
When the cycle is completed,
When man gets back to another and higher point of
equipoise,
Then at last he will know the why and wherefore of
it all.

III

While we walk together, brother, let us call another
comrade to join us.
See, he is coming toward us—he, the ultimate man
who will tread these paths at the end of the

cycle, four hundred or four thousand years
hence.

He presses in between us, and we three move on
together hand in hand.

What love and strength there are in his look and in
his gait!

We cannot take his measure, but he comprehends us
both.

He has all your vigorous out-door virtues, and mine
of the thoughtful fireside.

How he embraces us and sums us up and transcends
us!

I think that I read gratitude too in his eyes as he
gazes upon us.

He knows that we made him what he is:

That your childlike simplicity and instinctive
ferocity, that my morbid scruples and hair-
splitting philosophy were all steps up to
him.

If he could envy anyone, he might perhaps envy us
our creative influence ever widening down the
ages.

Come, my brothers, let us mutually interchange and
enjoy each others' functions and fruition.

For one brief hour let us plough and sow and culti-
vate and reap the harvest together.

Let us all share in common the eternal, divine manhood, in which we are really one.

Nor will it be only for an hour,
For I shall never walk these woods unaccompanied
    again.

Prophet, Priest, and King ❧

M AN is one.
    All ages are bound together.
The *is* grew out of the *was* and in turn becomes the
    will be.
We all travel the same road, in the same caravan;
    some before, some behind;
The prophet in the van linking us to the religion of
    the future,
The priest in the rear linking us to the religion of
    the past.
We trudge on between, looking forward or back-
    ward,
But forgetful, most of us, of the real religion
    above;
Blind to the eternal now, in which priest and prophet
    are at one together, united in the present
    king,
And where old types and symbols tally with the
    newest dreams.

Man ❧

" AND God created man in His own image."
What has become of that lost type?

If we could see it now reappearing, how would
that first ideal compare with yours and
mine?

In thousands of men and women—martyrs, heroes,
sages, poets, artisans, ploughmen, seamen,
soldiers, criminals, and outlaws—

We may gather his scattered lineaments and re-
construct him.

He must have the innocence and humility of the
saint, the power of self-conquest of the ascetic,
the broad vision of the seer, the loving-kindness of the lover of men,

The unquestioning devotion to quiet usefulness of
the labourer, the submission and the contempt
for danger of the sailor and trooper.

He must show the nonchalance of the gamester, the
geniality of the tippler, the easy manners of
the dissipated man of the world.

He must feel the absolute freedom, the revolt
against all external unassimilated law, of the
felon, the anarchist, and the atheist.

He must be endowed with all the intelligence,
strength, vigour, and energy of the un-

scrupulous captain of industry who relentlessly moulds the social forces to his will.

His must be the ambition, self-sufficiency, and
command of the proud ruler of armied states.

He must wield all the powers of selfishness and hate
under the supreme sway of an infinite com-
passion and love.

He must control these sinister forces in himself as a
Greek demi-god firmly planted on the back of
an unruly stallion.

There is no man or woman living who cannot con-
tribute some trait to the ideal, comprehensive
man.

There is no human note, high or low, which has not
its place in the wide scale of his being.

We are busy to-day fashioning this divine creature;

For the sun has not yet gone down on the sixth
creative day.

The sabbath of rest is still to come, if it ever
comes;

For the Father worketh even until now, and we
work.

We are His conscious partners in creating man in
His own image.

The Ball=Match ❧

I

WHY do respectability and refinement and
education and station present such deaden-
ing surfaces to me?

Even here in church, where they talk of communion
and unity, the fashionable congregation is a
mere chance collection of separate units.

If they are really in communication with heaven,
each worshipper must have a special wire.

As between themselves they are absolutely insulated;
for purple and fine linen are the surest spiritual
non-conductors.

Perhaps if there were patches on their trousers or
holes at their elbows some virtue might ooze
out of them or penetrate into them.

II

For my part, I find more real religion at a base-ball
match than in a Fifth Avenue church.

The good-natured crowd surges in when the gates
are opened, and soon the wooden benches are
black with people up to the highest tier.

Vendors of score-cards and refreshments cry their
wares.

The Ball-Match

Pea-nuts are in great demand, and the empty shells
    are scattered right and left.

The floor is not innocent of tobacco juice nor the
    air of profanity.

The game is called: a witty onlooker shouts out
    some bantering remark to one of the players,
    and all within sound of his voice laugh up-
    roariously.

The captain of the home team bats far afield and
    gains his base, while the whole crowd, fused
    into one by enthusiasm, rises to its feet with
    a tremendous cheer.

When the visitors score a well-deserved run there is
    applause too, but it is more reserved and
    measured, and we are conscious of our
    magnanimity.

There are constant cries of encouragement, of dis-
    appointment, of criticism of the umpire;

But the prevailing note is one of fellow-feeling, of
    common interest, of sympathy.

These are indeed vulgar wayside flowers, but from
    them the soul may distil honey.

When I think of the ball-match, St. Frigida's seems
    to me like an ice-house.

Orbits ❧

I LOVE you, just where you are,
But go no farther away and draw no closer.
When we are all whirling in our proper orbits,
How we exult in the forces that play between us,
Rioting with the centrifugal, plunging with the
centripetal,
And yet calm and unshaken in such a divine
equilibrium!
But oh, the derangement when we lose the just
balance and deviate from the way!
Here collisions, there explosions,
Death and havoc and hate!
Nay, even in the universe of love, there are respect-
ful distances to be observed,
If we are to have dignity and unity and harmony.

Love ❧

DO you complain that I do not love you as I
ought?
That if you should drop by the wayside I would
walk on and waste no time in useless
lamentation?

It is true and it is false.

In loving you I love more than you.

When I embrace you my arms encircle something
   vague and vast behind you.

When I gaze into the depths of your eyes I look
   beyond the farthest constellation.

You are not a finality; you are the way.

Through you and in you I love the whole world.

If you fall at my side, I know that you will still be
   walking by me.

If I fall myself, I shall only be the closer to you.

Why then should we be anxious, when we may
   live where there is neither separation nor
   death?

Love on a lower plane is but a brief illusion.

Do you Shrink ❧

DO you shrink at the idea of merging yourself
   in others?

Are you afraid of the shock? Is it like a cold
   plunge? Do you suppose that you will be
   submerged and lost?

Not so. You will not lose yourself in the universal,
   like the Buddhist, but it is there that you will
   find yourself.

Now, solitary, separate, unrelated, you are nothing;

The Great Mystery

When you think to stand alone, you are really not
    standing at all;
Yet with all your conceit and ambition you have
    not in your wildest dreams imagined what
    you might be.
Dash in boldly with your arms outstretched, and
    learn that you are a god.

The Great Mystery

I

IT does not satisfy, your philosophy.
    What is this energy oozing up into our being?
Does it grow, develop, evolve unguided, unpropelled,
Struggling on blindly from dead, dark beginnings
    in old chaos towards some central radiant
    fulfilment in the far-away ages to be?
Is my consciousness and yours its highest point
    to-day?
Does it nowhere else feel itself, question itself, know
    itself?
Is God then still to be waited for?
Nay, nay; this cannot be.

II

Ah, we who thread our narrow way through the
    infinite real,

Who must see in succession even the tiny portions
that we do see,
Who name our little journey "time," and put the
past before the future, because we entered by
the one door and are hastening on to the
other,
What do we know of eternity?

III

That which is growing is also full-grown.
That which is prophesied is.
The dream of the seer is more solid than earth.
The end was attained long, long ago, and the
beginning is yet to come.
Like shuttles, our little lives go on for ever weaving
the web and woof of the real;
Yet for ever the ideal was, filling the all.
Though no man hath seen the Father at any time,
Still His infinite self-consciousness inhabiteth eternity,
And eternally saith, "I am."

IV

Round the citadel of the eternal selfhood we are
bivouacked,
Most of us asleep at our posts, unmindful of our
great task to gain a foothold there.
Only here and there a stray company look for a
breach,

7   97

The Great Mystery

And succeed only by reversing their outer natures,
Abandoning all they have hitherto lived for,
Losing their life to find it.
The clinging, social, pliant Hindoo cuts himself off
     from his fellows, and lives as a hermit,
Strengthening his will until it becomes superhuman,
Mastering his thoughts and desires, treading his
     body in the dust;
At last passing in for a time, feeling the divine
     warm air surging about him,
Retaining only enough of self to feel the ineffable joy,
The feeble thus taking the kingdom of heaven by
     force.
His self-centred, self-reliant brother of the West
     meanwhile denies his outer nature too,
More slowly but more surely seeking admittance,
Forgetting himself, merging himself in his fellows,
     striving to love his neighbour,
Moving thus indirectly on the stronghold,
Destined perhaps to find the drawbridge down, the
     doors wide open,
The power of love supreme where will could but win
     a doubtful, transitory victory.

V

And in the moment of success in East and West
     alike, the mystery of sex strangely suggests
     itself,

The union of God and man in some way recalling
  the union of man and woman;
The same experience recorded in the earliest days,
  and typified in tabernacle and temple;—
Jehovah jealous of Israel, His spouse;
Osiris, the vine-grower, Isis, the giver of corn, leading
  the Egyptian mysteries hand in hand;
Bacchus and Ceres, wine and bread, wedded at
  Eleusis;
Christ and the Church, the bridegroom and the bride,
  again represented in the same elements at the
  great Christian feast.
Sex too at the centre of the Brahmin worship;
Saint and adept detecting the same passion in their
  religion.
Sex, in spite of all science, a great mystery,
Felt to-day in the sense of shame in his own person
  by the philosopher himself, who would sweep
  all mysteries away and all religion with them.

VI

Howbeit, this is our goal, to be put in touch with
  the universal consciousness, to find the hidden
  living bond between all, beneath all;
To recall the primal oneness, to realise the unity
  that is and ever shall be;
To know that whatever grand fruition the ages hold
  in store,

The Way and the End

The same was in the beginning with God.
This is the reality behind our little socialisms and
    communisms,
This the essence of religion and of life.

The Way and the End ❧

I

THE Way begins in the sense of sin, in self-
    abhorrence and renunciation, in acknowledged
    emptiness ;
It winds through self-denial, through submission
    and meekness and humility, through patience
    and long-suffering ;
It leads us up higher, past the forgiveness of others
    and the acceptance of them upon their own
    terms ;
Such is the Way, but it is not the End.

II

The End is the consciousness of the heaven-born
    selfhood ;
The new self, found and loved in eternal fellowship ;
The self-centred, self-sufficient pride of divine man-
    hood ;
The glad fulness of exultant, unbounded, everlasting,
    almighty love.

The Seed ❧

THE seed is the magician of life.
    Dropped into the dead soil of the field or
    of our souls,
It draws the inert matter into its mysterious moulds,
Transforms it into a living thing of beauty,
And sends up its flowering miracle to the light of
    day,
Opening for us a channel even unto heaven.
It subdues easiest the vilest rotting humus, — the
    publican and the sinner,—
And is baffled only by the stony pride of scribe
    and Pharisee.
It is a winged particle of the central life,
Sent forth to spread that life, and, spreading it, to
    make all things new.

Initiation ❧

I

IT is a glorious thing to be really alive,—
    To feel one's self a co-operating agent in the
    mysterious business of the universe,—
To be admitted as a member of the gigantic
    trust,—

Initiation

To be initiated into the central labour union of
   all,—
Once for all to be let into the secrets of the cosmic
   conspiracy.

II

Yon star winks down at me and gives me the pre-
   concerted sign ;
The woodpecker drums the password on a resonant
   dead bough ;
I return their signals and hail them both as
   brothers.
For are we not all engaged in the self-same
   enterprise ?
Do we not get our impulse from the same general
   headquarters ?

III

Nor is ours an exclusive combine.
We do not measure our privileges from any outside
   penury.
We wish to leave nothing outside.
Our only message to you who insist on staying
   without is the persistently reiterated, persistently rejected invitation to come in on
   the ground-floor.

The Ladder of Truth ❧

SIN, justice, fear, an angry Judge—with these we are on the lowest round of the ladder of truth.

How long the world dwelt there, and how many still look back regretful to those days!

One step higher and we find forgiveness and a Father.

For most men that is the last word, but we must press upward.

Beyond fatherhood and brotherhood we grope toward organic oneness—we dimly feel that God is palpitating, all-embracing love.

Truth Again ❧

SECRETE truth in your intellect, and you will find it a heavy burthen.

There it will only cloy and glut and obstruct.

Truth is not food for knowledge but for life.

You must love the truth and feel the truth and assimilate the truth.

What you need is not truth known but truth lived.

Truth cannot be stored away without ceasing to be truth;

It cannot be idle without becoming a lie.

Self=Denial 🐌

GIVE up nothing so long as you can help giving
it up.

Do not deny yourself until self insists on being
denied.

Let the flood of rebellion against selfishness gather
above the dam till it sweeps all before it.

Gorge yourself with quails until you loathe them.

When at last luxury and privilege and authority fill
you with disgust,

Then seek out the poor, because you cannot do
otherwise ;

Become satisfied with your simple manhood, because
you have learned that it is the sum of all
possessions.

Be Still 🐌

BE still, my soul.
Rest awhile from the feverish activities in
which you lose yourself.

Be not afraid to be left alone with yourself for one
short hour.

Aspire upward, inward, until, as from a mountain top,
you have a glimpse over all the world.

See the little fields in which men toil, ignorant of all
beyond the hedge ;

There but a few minutes ago you were rushing to
and fro.

Look forth now and fix upon your memory the
great outlines of God's kingdom ;

Store up within you the treasures of that outlook,

And then descend once more with shining face into
the plain.

Let it be your task henceforward to externalise the
secrets of that vision. ╱

Beware 🐌

HAVE you always been respected by your
neighbours?

Do they ask your advice on all important matters ?

Do they all speak well of you, and point you out as
a leading citizen and a pillar of society ?

Has no one ever said that you were beside yourself,

Or called you crazy, or a crank, or a pestilent fellow ?

Have you never been accused of associating with
publicans and sinners, or of stirring up the
people, or of turning the world upside down ?

Not I

In short, are you thoroughly respectable?
Then beware! you are on the downward road; you
    are in bad company.
Mend your ways, or you can claim no kinship with
    the saints and heroes which were before
    you. /

Not I ❧

OH, I love mankind, as is their due,
    With all my might and main.
It is true that I sometimes seem to do
A rather unloving thing or two,
    But it always gives me pain.

Thus it is when I can't give a debtor time
    On a mortgage he's trying to lift.
But you see, so far from being a crime,   --
It's a duty—and duties are all sublime—
    To foreclose and turn him adrift.

And it's easy enough for me to show
    The innocence of my act.
It was not as myself that I acted so,
(For I never would hurt a fly, you know),
    But just as attorney-in-fact.

Not I

While the unemployed are with us still,
　　My soul is quite dejected.
I only vote for the Tariff Bill,
That closes many a German mill,
　　As a senator elected.

'Tis true, I once looted a poor man's farm
　　And burnt his house to boot;
But the fact is, I only did him harm
(And my heart the while was intensely warm)
　　As a cavalry recruit.

And once again I condemned a youth
　　To be hanged in the early morn;
But I did it not as myself forsooth,
(You must admit that I tell the truth),
　　But as judge commissioned and sworn.

And when I declare the rents too low,
　　It is only as trustee.
You may blame me as agent of Richard Roe,
As director, official, or so and so,
　　But never at all as me.

Still the question will arise unbid,
　　" Is there aught, since my life began,
That I ever do or ever did
(If there is, it has been most deftly hid)
　　As a plain and simple man?"

Lex Talionis

And it surely is very odd to see
   The effect of our point of view.
It's a curious plan, you must agree,
While *you* do my dirty work for me,
   That I should do yours for you.

Brothers of mine, if we might all
   Have our lives to live over again :
If every deed we might recall,
And never do anything, great or small,
   That we would not do as men—

Then at last our conscience would begin
   To show us its native powers,
And how much of pain and sorrow and sin,
And crime, confusion and strife and din,
   Would be spared this world of ours !

Lex Talionis 🍂

" AN eye for an eye and a tooth for a tooth."
   This great law has never been abrogated,
and we still pray, " Forgive us our debts,
as we forgive our debtors."
Forgiveness alone begets forgiveness.
In some form you must render the eye and the
   tooth, even if it be but in the relinquishment

of your just claim to the eye and tooth of
another.

The law still lives, but, thank God, you and I are
not the executioners.

Who hath made us to be judges between men?

Like all true laws, it executes itself.

We reap what we sow, but it is not ours to interfere
with our neighbour's harvest.

" Vengeance is Mine; I will repay," saith the
Lord

The Regiment ❧

I

THE regiment is passing down the street to
embark for the war.

The band is playing a stirring, swelling march.

The colonel rides alone, with the easy excellence
and mastery of a perfect horseman on a
perfect horse.

The rank and file march proudly by with eyes fixed
before them.

There is conscious courage and self-sacrifice in their
look.

Their bayonets are glancing in the sun.

The Regiment

The crowd on each side is carried away with
    enthusiasm, hurrahing, waving handkerchiefs
    and hats, and some even shedding tears.
It is indeed a thrilling sight.
I stand at a window disapproving, and yet the
    excitement beats up against me and over-
    whelms me.
It is fine; it is grand; it is splendid!
I wave my handkerchief with the rest, and my eyes
    too become moist.

III

And yet I know what these men are advancing to.
They will slaughter other men as courageous and
    self-sacrificing as themselves, and against
    whom they have no grievance.
They will grasp others as lovable by the throat in a
    death struggle, and one life or the other will
    go out in hate.
They will fill a distant land with moanings and
    groanings and torments, with widows and
    orphans.
They will do all this and more, and yet I am forced
    unwillingly to feel that there is something
    magnificent in their spirit and carriage.

IV

What baleful influence has thus mingled the good
with the evil ?

How come God and the devil to be thus inextricably
intertwined ?

Ah, it is the riddle of the age, to separate these
contrary principles of life and death,

To stamp out all that is cruel and diabolical, without
treading on the smallest atom of divine
manliness and devotion.

Must we wait long for a heaven-born solution ?

God forbid ! but meanwhile I stand at my window,
waving my handkerchief with shame and
hesitation.

The New Commandment ❧

I

L IVE in others ;
    Have life abundantly, but have it in the
circle of the beloved.

Bathe yourself with rapture in the crowd on the
street ;

Let the bath in the unwashed, unkempt, elbowing
multitude be to you as a dip in the sea,

The New Commandment

For it purifies the soul as the salt, heaving ocean
purifies.

Let your attitude to all men be one of continual
embrace.

So do, and death will not know where to find you.

II

These expressions of love to your fellows,—

The glad eye, the hand-shake, the evident content,—

They but reflect a new truth at the bottom of your
soul.

Do your branches spread out among the boughs of
the forest?

So, in equal measure, your hidden, mysterious roots
are feeling their way.

There in the depths is the source of all;

There you are stretching out to God;

There you find the message that you bear to your
neighbour.

Your chief significance lies in this, that you help
bind your neighbour to God, as he in turn
may help to bind you.

It is thus that you complete the magnetic circuit of
the universe, and share in the all-vibrating
Love.

Life's Tragedy ❧

I

THE loneliness of souls
    Talking of companionship and brother-
    hood, but finding them not;
Praying that others may be one with them,
But the others stoutly refusing to comply,
And in the hour of trial forsaking and fleeing;
And then the still sharper pang of disappointment,
    as we long for the abstract unity of all,
And yet surprise our very selves in the act of
    rebelling before the concrete case;
Filled with disgust at another's trivial fault;
Refusing to pour forth our treasures for him;
Doubtful even if we have treasures to pour forth;
Aware of unsounded depths of malice and loveless-
    ness within;
Feeling perhaps less brotherly than those who have
    no glorious dreams—
This, this is the tragedy of conscious human life!

II

Those who live unconsciously,
Ignorant of their own limitations,
Blind to the wall that hems them in in solitary
    confinement,

8   113

After the Procession

Touching others at the rim, and knowing nothing
of the possibility of closer contact ;
Unmindful of sources and roots, and the attraction
and heat and light of invisible solar orbs ;
Paralysed and numb at the very centre—
Who shall say that their fate is not even more tragic ?

After the Procession ❧

I

AN hour has passed since the procession has
vanished down the avenue.
The crowd which had waited expectant from early
morning has at last melted away.
They went as they came, down the side streets east
and west, to their teeming tenements in the
direction of the river fronts.
Working men, women, children, and babes in arms—
All day long they were huddled together on the
brown stone stoops of the fine houses along
the line of march,
Or else stood patiently on the curb, scarcely restrained
by the rows of policemen.
Now they have all gone, weary and sated, to their
homes,
Leaving behind them the marks of their unwonted
incursion.

After the Procession

Cigar stumps, greasy brown paper, redolent of ham
    sandwiches and cheese, rubbish of many kinds,
    pollute the proud doorsteps and area-ways
    and litter the side-walk.

Contemptuous butlers and housemaids emerge to
    sweep and scour away every vestige of the
    plebeian merry-making;

All will soon be clean again, and the atmosphere
    sweet once more to our nostrils.

II

We pray for salvation, and fail to recognise it at our
    very doors.

These crowds bring the purest, life-giving mountain
    air to our souls, and we turn away.

Not reluctantly but gladly should we admit them,
    not only to our threshold but to the holy of
    holies of our heart.

The refuse which they strew about, these offences to
    our over-nice ears and eyes and noses, are but
    vulgar illusions.

Who knows how much good, how much of joyful
    experience, we sweep away with them?

Let us open our doors, throw down our area railings,
    and allow the rabble to surge in to our inner-
    most selves;

For this is the price of salvation and of life.

If we stop short of this, we shall never have lived.

The Friar and the Devil ❧

I

I THANK God that I am a friar of the order of
St. Francis,

For he never forgets his little brothers;

And without him how should I ever have subdued
the devil?

Ay, for the devil worried me sorely.

Not that I did not know what true life was;

For had I not felt the holy ecstasy,

The profound flow within from the waist upward,

Lifting me till my very feet no longer touched the
ground,

And filling me with love for every creature?

But that was only now and again, when I had done
some little act of kindness, or when I knelt
gazing long at the picture of the Blessed
Virgin in my cell.

Ah, the devil knows when to strike, and at such times
he left me alone;

But in the tiresome stretches between he watched his
chances.

And when he hits he does not fight fairly, for he
always hits below the belt,

Drawing the current of life downward, until the whole
man sinks in the mire.

So I prayed to St. Francis, but for a time he came
not.

And I thought to myself, " How strange it is that I
should really be the vilest man on earth;

If people saw my thoughts and imaginations how
they would abhor me."

For it was true then that the devil had my mind fast
in his toils,

Except that I still prayed to St. Francis.

II

Now on the eve of the Second of August,

The great day on which he offers us absolution each
year,

I prayed to him harder than ever, feeling that he
must come now;

And I went to sleep peacefully and full of hope.

And behold, he did come, looking for all the world
like the picture in the refectory, with the holes
in the back of his hands and an angel over
each shoulder, and he held a scroll with a text
on it before him.

And I cried, " Oh, good St. Francis, do kill the devil
and lift me up to the holy life again."

But he looked very solemn, and the angels seemed
quite shocked, and he said:

" I would fain lift thee up, but I cannot kill the devil."

Then my heart fainted within me.

The Friar and the Devil

" What can I do, dear Saint ? " I sighed. " Who can
    help me, if not thou ? "
And then he smiled, and said :
" Thou should'st ask our little brother the devil to
    help lift thee up."
And then the angels smiled too.
And with these words on his lips he slowly faded
    away, and I got up and wrote them down
    while they were still in my ears.
And then indeed they frightened me, for if St.
    Francis had not uttered them himself, and if
    the angels had not smiled, I should have said
    that they were rank heresy, which God forbid.

III

But I could not doubt our own good Saint.
And when the devil came again that self-same night,
    instead of trying to grasp him by the throat,
    as I was wont to do, I looked at him kindly,
    and said :
" Dear little brother, do not pull me down any
    farther ; but lend me thy shoulder and push
    me up, and let that wonderful vigour of thine
    run up through me towards heaven and not
    downwards to the mire."
And while I was still speaking, I saw the devil no
    longer, but I felt the old ecstasy, only a
    thousandfold stronger than ever ; and I loved

God and all created things as never before,
and my soul seemed to soar in the air.
And now the joy abides with me, and every day I
thank St. Francis that he did not slay the devil.

The Wise and Foolish Seeds ↝

I

TWIN seeds lay together in the warm womb of
the garden.

From one of them a tiny shoot sped upward and
another downward.

" Beware," cried the down-shoot to his fellow ; " you
are going in the wrong direction. I know that
I am right ; I feel it in my inmost sap. Mother
Earth is calling us down to her ; turn back
from your mad career."

" Nay," responded the up-shoot ; " it is you who are
at fault. The sun is beckoning to us from
above ; push up to the surface of the ground
with me. We cannot both be right, and I am
sure of my own course."

And so they wrangled until they both doubted, and
their strength was wasted in argument and
conjecture ; and the growing days passed by
unimproved, and the frost came, and the seed
died without having seen the daylight.

II

And in like manner two shoots made their appear-
ance in the other seed.

" Farewell, my brother," said one to the other ;

" Follow your call, and I will follow mine, and so we
shall both work together for the good of all."

And each went his way, the one sucking up the riches
of the soil and passing them up to the stem,
and the other drinking in the air and sunlight
and sending them down to the root.

And there grew from that seed a beautiful red-
flowering shrub, which filled the air with its
perfume and scattered its seeds in due time to
the winds.

Shine like the Sun ❧

SHINE like the sun on one and all, on the evil
and on the good, on the just and on the unjust, on the obliging and on the disobliging,
on them that love and on them that hate.

This is no sign of weakness or foolishness, of a mean
spirit or of fear.

It but shows our near relation to the source of all
force and light and heat and life ;

It proves the inexhaustible resources of the mighty
reservoir on which we draw.

Whither and Whence? ⮞

WHITHER and whence?
How the old world of matter goes travel-
ling through me atom by atom,
Coming I know not whence,
Sojourning with me for a day or a week or a year,
Coursing in my blood, camping out in my flesh and
bone, and then off again I know not whither,
Leaving its old familiar mask behind it, as if to say,
So much for your identity.

Whither and whence?
The world of spirit too glides through me—
Dreams, thoughts, affections, aspirations, whether I
wake or sleep ;
Now asserting themselves peremptorily,
Now in gentler mood letting themselves be marshalled
and subordinated,
But always on the march,
Coming from one land of mystery and hastening on
to another.

Whither and whence?
Here I stand nicely balanced at the cross roads,
The two processions ever traversing each other with-
out noise or jostle ;

Whither and Whence?

Here I stand toiling day and night to put up a sign-
post,
Asking the passers-by in vain the whence and
whither.
They pursue their journey without turning their faces,
and leave me none the wiser.

Whither and whence?
The simple folk of old had their sign-post.
Where the roads crossed they lifted up another cross ;
It meant the divine crossing the human in love,
Joining it, and henceforth wedded to it, making it
whole ;
Its arms not marking north and south and east and
west,
But pointing from back forward and from down up—
Upward and onward ; ✓
Setting up this quadrant to measure the heavens by,
So far definite, but beyond still leaving the mystery.
This was the sign-post of the wise, simple folk of old,
The cross at the crossing where you and I are toil-
ing.
Will ours be truer or clearer ?

Whither and whence?
Henceforth I ask that question no more.
The two processions still pass by, making the sign
of the cross themselves for me.

They are the question and they are the answer.

Here meet and unite spirit and matter, heaven and
earth, God and man;

Here if anywhere must I look for wisdom and goodness, faith and love.

Here, just where I stand, is the centre of all the
worlds;

Here come together the great highways of the universe.

Do I ask, *Whither and whence?*
Nay, it is all hither and hence.
This is the goal and the starting-point.
Let the clouds rest upon the margins;
Whatever happens there, I am secure.
My post is here and now.

Ring out, ye Bells ❧

I

RING out, ye playful bells,—playful, yet serious
bells,—

For to-day is my wedding-day.

Call in from the streets and lanes of the city, and
from the highways and hedges,

The poor and the maimed and the halt and the
blind;

123

Ring out, ye Bells

All must be bidden and all must needs come,
For the whole creation is my bride.

II

Ring out, ye bells!
I am in love with all—spirit and flesh, earth and sky,
mountain and sea.
That which is I, wedded to that which is not I,
makes up the whole universe.
I am as necessary to it as it is to me.
Neither of us can spare the other;
We are suited to each other; we were made for
each other;
No pair of twin indentures ever fitted so closely.

III

Ring out, ye bells!
We two were put asunder, but that we might be
joined again.
Along our common frontier is all the give and take,
all the interchange and play of forces of the
worlds.
The thrill of the separation, the thrill of the re-
union, this is life;
It will never cease again; the new oneness will have
gained a new life.
Ring on, ye bells,—playful and serious bells,—
Ring on now for ever.

Blossoms ~&

WHEN in April the cherry trees spring into bloom,

And the blossoms cluster thick like white butterflies on the bare branches,

They all don their gay uniform together; not one lags behind.

The same impulse at the same moment stirs the old trees in the garden, and the wild cherry trees in the woods across the road.

The early birds and insects gather to them, and hail their fragrance with cheerful chirp and hum.

A week later comes the time of the pear trees, and their life bursts forth simultaneously everywhere.

Our orchard displays its colours as at the word of command.

On the far hillside we see other orchards aligned like battalions of infantry.

The solitary pear tree by the door forgets not its duty, and signals back to the others.

And now, while the pear blossoms fall, the apple trees bring up their reinforcements, and their

blossoms break out in the midst of the young
green leaves.

The apple tree in the pear orchard has made no
mistake; it has bided its time, and now lets
itself go with its brethren.

What subtle, palpitating bond has drawn these trees
together in sympathy?

Whence is the magnetic thrill to which each in its
turn responds?

II

The world of souls hath its seasons of bloom likewise.

Nay, one of them is even now upon us.

Are you not conscious of the new love-blossom un-
folding within you,

The blossom of fellowship with man, of a wider,
closer communion?

Look forth on distant lands, and see on every hand
the same delicate flower here and there ap-
pearing.

We feel the same mystic bond; we yield to the
same inexplicable thrill.

There have been other blooming times and other
blossoms;

We rejoice that it was so, and have no quarrel with
those who came before us.

But now at last it is our day; we feel the sap within
us, we mutually recognise the tint and the
perfume, the joy of life and of reproduction is
ours.

We foresee that at the great harvest-home our rosy,
mellow fruit will be gathered in in basketfuls
with the rest.

The Great Joy 〜

I

THERE is one joy which soars and hovers above
all other joys,

And your hands are not free to grasp it until you
drop the lesser joys.

Then at last you learn its secret, for lo! it contains
all the others and sums them up.

Each individual joy is there; not one is lacking.

II

Seek the great joy.

To do it, let slip your wealth and your dreams of
wealth.

What miracle is this? You have thus become the
possessor of all the earth,

And for the first time you can really enjoy your
heritage.

The Great Joy

You have risen above the region of exclusive riches,
    and now all things are yours.

III

Renounce your ability to command and to look
    down upon your fellows.
Give up your schemes of political and social ambi-
    tion ;
And behold, you find yourself at once near the
    source of all power,
One of the elect few of all the ages,
Sharing in the creative forces of the world,
Your will in some way, to some extent, a part of the
    Divine will.

IV

Resign, if need be, the one most loved of all ;
Waive your claims, assert no selfish prerogative ;
And again on a higher plane your love embraces all.
Now in the all you possess the loved one, who in
    turn through the all must now love you and
    delight in you.
In that upper air there is no escape from you.

V

Let your life and all its aims go ;
Make it so cheap that you can quite disregard it.

And lo, once more you are lifted up to the centre of
the universe;
The all-life, the life eternal, with all its treasures,
becomes your own.
You have lost your life, and you have found it.
Yours at last is the great joy.

Talium est enim
Regnum Coelorum ❧

I

A HOT, dusty crowd has gathered in the railway
station, and is elbowing its way through the
funnel at the door while the porter punches
the tickets.
The hour-glass is filled with unruly, unnatural human
sand,
Dropping its anxious, questioning, uncomfortable
grains one by one on the platform.
But a little child joins the throng and is sucked
into the vortex.
A way is opened for him.
Men and women whose faces showed a moment
ago no trace of aught but the sharpening,
narrowing struggle for existence, begin at last
to smile.

9

Talium est enim Regnum Coelorum

One strokes the little fellow's head, another play-
    fully pulls his ear, a third shows him where
    to present his ticket;
Even the busy doorkeeper finds time for a friendly
    wink.
The travellers interchange glances, and are almost
    ashamed that their naked moral selves have
    been exposed to view.
But it is too late; the magic deed has been done.
For an instant the boy has crystallised those repellent
    atoms of sand into a beautiful unity,
And the little wizard has passed on, unconscious of
    his work.

II

Ah me, what goodness lies buried in every human
    soul, waiting for the enchanter's wand!
We were each of us wizards once.
We were born such, and for a few brief years we
    went about turning hearts of stone into hearts
    of flesh.
How did we lose the happy art?
How did we sink so low as to need its ministrations
    for ourselves?
Can we not regain the subtle power?
At least let us open our souls to its influence, and
    perchance it may revive a kindred force
    within us.

What function is there nobler than the calling forth
of what is best in others? ✓

What career grander than that which devotes us to
such a mission?

What triumph more sublime than the opening
flowers which greet each ray of the rising
sun?

The Old, Old Quest ❧

I

WHY are the people thronging up the steps of
the grey cathedral? What makes them
so anxious, so eager, so impetuous?

It is the old, old quest. They are looking for life
eternal.

Who is that tall cloaked figure that treads stealthily
behind them?

It is Death. See, they feel his presence, and they
dare not turn their heads lest they should
behold him.

II

The procession of priests is marching solemnly up
the aisle. As they pass us, we note the hope-
ful faces of those who are still young, and the
stolid or despairing looks of the old men.

The Old, Old Quest

How dim the light is! We can hardly see
that they have reached the chancel.

What are they searching for now under the altar
and behind the bishop's throne?

It is the old, old quest. They are looking for life
eternal.

Who is that tall cloaked figure that treads stealthily
behind them?

It is Death. See, they feel his presence, and they
dare not turn their heads lest they should
behold him.

III

The aged man is bending over a great book. He
is alone in his study, and shelf on shelf of
well-worn volumes rises behind him.

He takes up his goose-quill. How fast he writes!
The floor is strewn with sheets of foolscap
closely written, and now again he is fumbling
over the yellow printed pages.

He cannot find the text he is seeking. I
wonder why he is thus straining his poor
red eyes?

It is the old, old quest. He is looking for life
eternal.

But he is not alone. Who is that tall cloaked
figure stooping over his shoulder?

It is Death. See, he feels his presence, and he dare not turn his head lest he should behold him.

IV

A sister of charity is dying on her straw pallet. She lovingly nursed back the life of the fever-stricken tramp, though she knew that she was drinking in the poison.

Here is work for our old friend Death. Where is his tall cloaked figure?

Ah, he is not here! and the sister smiles, for she knows that he cannot enter.

How can she, in her agony, be happy?

Do you not understand? She holds the clue to the old, old quest, though she never sought it, for she feels throbbing in her innermost soul the forces of life eternal.

The New Creation 🙶

THE world to-day is without form and void, and darkness is upon the face of the deep.

But lo! the Spirit of Love moveth upon the face of the waters of humanity,

And we shall ere long see a new heaven and a new earth.

And behold, it will be very good.

Good and Evil ❧

GOOD without evil?   Oh, vain, vain dream!
   Pleasure without pain, light without shadow,
   heaven without hell?
We cannot trifle thus with the eternal balances.
We can only paint our paradise on the eternal back-
   ground.
We cannot lift the earth without a resting-point for
   our lever.
God Himself can but divide the light from the dark-
   ness.
He can polarise the forces of life, but He cannot
   annihilate that without which life is impossible;
For even the Almighty hath His " must."
But though we suffer let us rejoice in the eternal
   equilibrium, for it is ours.

The Experiment ❧

THE book said, " Love others; love them calmly,
   strongly, profoundly,
And you will find your immortal soul."
I leaned back in my arm-chair, letting my hand fall
   with the volume in my lap,

And with closed eyes and half a smile on my face
I made the experiment and tried to love.
For the first time I really let my life go forth in love,
and lo, the mighty current, welling up beneath
and around me, lifted me, as it were bodily,
out of time and space.
I felt the eternal poise of my indestructible soul in
the regions of life everlasting.
Immortality was mine.
The question which had so long baffled the creeds
and the philosophers was answered.

The White Soul ✥

I SAW Innocence oppressed, and I pitied and
loved her;
And I looked upon my soul, and it was radiantly
white, like unto the noonday sun.
Then I was moved to seize the Oppressor and slay
him ;
And as I watched my soul it became red and angry
and troubled, even as the setting sun in a
stormy sky.
And I grieved for its lost glory, and envied the state
of those who might still possess it ; and I saw
my soul that it became green like a sickly
moon.

Everlasting Habitations

So I lifted up my voice and prayed, and said, "O
Lord, cast all these lurid and unhealthy
passions out from my soul."

And behold, there was a great darkness, and my soul
hung, black as a pall, in the midst of it.

Thereupon I wept bitterly, and cried, "O Lord, give
me back the glory."

And a voice answered and said, "Then thine must
be the passions also."

And I was carried away by love again, and once
more I saw the white radiance of my soul;
and my eyes were opened, and I beheld in
the blinding whiteness the rainbow of all the
passions transfigured and absorbed in the
magic flame of love.

And the voice said, "See to it that no passion
break forth again from its place in the perfect
circle."

Everlasting Habitations ❧

YE unjust stewards with your unjust wealth,
Keeping for yourselves the good things
that were meant for all,
Gladly let them slip through your fingers;
Give lovingly to him that asketh;
Make friends with the riches of unrighteousness;

And then, when ye are discharged from your post in
 this world,—
When at last ye seem to die,—
Then they, the poor, humble recipients of your
 bounty,
Will receive you into everlasting habitations.
In them will ye find eternal life.

The Search ❧

N O one could tell me where my Soul might be.
 I searched for God but God eluded me.
I sought my Brother out, and found all three.

Sapphics ❧

Y EARNING, oh, how drear is this endless
 yearning
After glory, love, power, wealth, achievement!
Fools, we long each one for his sep'rate pleasure,
 Careless of others.

Oft we fall and fail in our eager onset.
If we grasp the fruit, in our hand it shrivels;

Waiting

Soon we heave a sigh, for our soul is sated,
      Sick at the surfeit.

Ah, we thought these things in themselves were
      final,—
Took them all to heart as the end of effort.
Thus to make means ends is the old forbidden
      Worship of idols.

No, not ends,—these boons that we faint and strive
      for,—
Sign-posts rather, set to direct us onward;
Steps up which to climb to a height above, but
      Never to sit on;

Telescopes through which we may study heaven,
Their transparent help for the time forgetting;
Doors that lead us on to the Universal,
      If we but open.

Waiting

HOW long shall I be stifled in myself?
    I feel my kinship to the babe in the
womb, blindly elbowing his way to light for
his eyes and air for his lungs.
The kernel in the seed too is my cousin, swelling

madly under the turf at the inspired suggestion
of sunlight.

I know likewise that there is a Sun somewhere.

I strain and push, but perhaps I am straining and
pushing in the wrong direction.

I must wait in my tiny, outgrown cell.

No one knows better than I do how narrow I am,
but how can I be broad?

No one loves better than I do the wide, elemental
men, but they are not to be imitated.

I wait impatiently for the call to join them and be
one of them.

The Higher Trigonometry ❧

WOULD you find God in the heavens? Then
you must learn the rules of the celestial
trigonometry.

You have been trying all these years to draw a line
to Him from yourself alone, but no one can
measure the sky with one point as a base.

Get your other point first: find your brother; lay
down your base-line to him; establish your
angles from your mutual aspirations and
affections, and you have the problem solved.

√ No man cometh unto the Father save by the Son of
Man.

William Lloyd Garrison 🙽

I

IT is late in the evening.

 In a dingy attic room by the feeble light of a lamp a young workman of resolute and engaging countenance is setting up type for the first number of his journal.

An old-fashioned hand-press stands behind him; the floor is bespattered with printer's ink.

The type is worn and second-hand; the paper was bought on credit; the rent is unpaid; the youthful editor has neither money nor influence nor friends, nor as yet a single subscriber.

At his elbow his supper awaits him—a loaf of bread and a glass of milk, the only food he can afford to buy.

When he has finished his day's work, he will sleep there on the floor in the corner.

The world outside is thinking of presidents and senates and elections.

Lost on false trails, it recks not that in that humble chamber is being enacted much of the contemporary history of mankind.

It has still to learn that it must look in lowly mangers for the promise of the new day.

II

The young printer smiles confidently as he goes on
    with his work.

Here are the words which he is forming at the
    case :

" The standard of emancipation is now unfurled.

Let all the enemies of the persecuted blacks tremble.

I will be as harsh as truth and as uncompromising as
    justice.

I am in earnest.

I will not equivocate ;

I will not excuse ;

I will not retreat a single inch ;

And *I will be heard.*

Posterity will bear testimony that I was right."

For thirty long years he bears this standard aloft.

Mobbed by the people, imprisoned by the State, cast
    out by the churches ;

Dogged by kidnappers and assassins, a price set upon
    his head, despised, hated, and reviled ;

The wealth, learning, and religion of the land especi-
    ally bitter against him ;

He presses forward unmoved.

Scorning all compromise, deaf to every suggestion
    in extenuation, he lifts his voice like thunder
    above all other sounds,

Blasting for ever the man-stealer and his abettors.

William Lloyd Garrison

And at last, as he foresaw from the first, in loneliness and want—victory, complete victory, is
his.

III

In Garrison the truth conquered, the simple truth,
that " man cannot own his fellow."

There is another truth as simple waiting for its
sponsor, the truth that " the land belongs to
all."

Where is the man who will replace the fallen
champion of the landless ?

Where is the hero with hands clean of complicity,
with unbridled tongue, with withering contempt for all excuses, ready for a generation,
if need be, to lead on, through good and evil
report, through persecution and even unto
death, against the land-lords as Garrison did
against the man-lords ?

The times call out for such an one.

We, temporisers of all shades, shall recognise in him
our superior when he comes ;

To his standard we must unfalteringly rally.

Till then, no one need be fearful for his unearned
gains, though the world starve.

Choir Practice ❧

A S I sit on a log here in the woods among
the clean-faced beeches,
The trunks of the trees seem to me like the pipes
of a mighty organ,
Thrilling my soul with wave on wave of the
harmonies of the universal anthem—
The grand, divine, æonic " I am " chorus.
The red squirrel scolding in yonder hickory tree,
The flock of blackbirds chattering in council over-
head,
The monotonous crickets in the unseen meadow,
Even the silent ants travelling their narrow highway
with enormous burdens at my feet—
All, like choristers, sing in the green-arched cathedral
The heaven-prompted mystery, " I am, I am."
The rays of sunshine shoot down through the
branches and touch the delicate ferns and the
blades of coarse grass piercing up through
last year's dead leaves,
And all cry out together, " I am."
We used to call upon all these works of the Lord to
praise the Lord, and they did praise Him ;
But now they praise no longer, for they have been
taught a new song, and with one accord they
chant the " I am."

The Master

I too would learn the new music, and I begin
    hesitatingly to take part in the world-wide
    choir practice.
After all these quiet private rehearsals,
At last in my own place you may look for me also
    in the final, vast, eternal chorus.
And we, all of us, as you see us, are but mouth-
    pieces.
Who is it that behind and beneath sings ever through
    us, now whispering, now thundering, "I am"?

The Master 〰

THERE are times when I could thank God for
    the healthy paganism in the gospel.
It is only in that current of native vigour that our
    Christian virtues can ride supreme.
Does the Master walk in peace? He does it on a
    threatening, boisterous sea.
I like to see Him confounding the money-brokers
    with a glance as He upsets their tables, or else
    thundering at the respectable church people,
    or answering the Jewish archbishop with
    magnificent disdain.
All *that* was in Him.
When He said, "Suffer little children to come unto
    Me," all that was in Him.

When the beloved disciple lay with his head upon
   His breast, all that was in Him.
In the agony of the cross, while His weight bore
   down upon the burning nails, and He
   cried, " Father, forgive them," all that was
   in Him.
He was the Son of God, and called upon us to be
   sons of God—
Sons of the God of the tempest as well as the God
   of the calm.
The storm was in Him.
The passionate strength was in Him.
But, above all, on the very thunder-cloud, He wrote,
   " Peace, be still."
On any other parchment—in the mouths of blood-
   less saints and philosophers—those culminat-
   ing words lose all their force.
We need life, and we need it more abundantly.

At the Solicitor's 🙢

A FAIR young girl,
      Made by nature for the true life of woods
   and fields,
Or, if detained indoors,
Meant to form an incomparable picture,

At the Solicitor's

Standing with cheeks aglow and fresh apron before
    the kitchen fire,
Or singing as she sits at her needlework—

Such she was; but I sighed as I saw her in her
    lawyer's office,
Going over the accounts of her estate,
Discussing bonds and mortgages and other invest-
    ments,
Drawing cheques and signing receipts.
I wonder if she noticed my profound disgust?
Was I the only one there with eyes open to the
    monstrosity of it all?
Did I alone perceive, in this unthinking maiden,
    womanhood profaned and humanity blas-
    phemed?
Could no one else detect on that bright face the
    appalling taint of property?

I saw it indeed, and was shocked—
I, who can still behold unmoved those of my own
    sex engaged in such degrading business;
But the angels of heaven, who know full well what
    a human soul should be, can they look upon
    any of us without tears?

All Ye that Labour

"ALL ye that labour, come to Me,"
　　The Galilean Workman cried;
"Alone ye never can be free,
But, heavy laden though ye be,
　　The yoke seems nothing at My side.

"Love one another; do not stand
　　Forgetful of each other's woe;
Together seek the promised land;
Whate'er befall, clasp hand in hand,
　　And hold no brother for a foe.

"Together lay your treasure by,
　　And not in hoards of foolish gold;
But rather pile your riches high,
Of brother-love that cannot die,
　　And peace and mutual good untold.

"Behold the lilies of the plain
　　And all the birds that skim the air;
They have no barns to store the grain,
But, scorning ownership and gain,
　　They take their fill without a care.

"And so the day might pass for you
　　Without a single anxious thought,

The Workers to the Landlords

If each of you were only true
To all the rest, and strove to do
        The nearest service as he ought.

" Then, ever shining, like the sun,
        On them that love and them that hate,
Forgiving, loving everyone,
Soon would ye see My reign begun,
        My kingdom that ye must create.

" Come unto Me for rest and ease ;
        And where to find Me, would ye ask ?
Close by you is the arm that frees ;
Come, find Me in the least of these
        My brethren, toiling at his task."

The Workers to the Landlords &

O YE who say ye own the land,
        Where is the grant that blessed you thus ?
Who gave you mountain, plain, and strand ?
        The God that made the land made us.

He made us, and we till His soil ;
        We work His mines and fell His trees ;
In stone and iron and wood we toil.
        Your titles, are they more than these ?

The Workers to the Landlords

We earn our bread with sweating brow ;
   Ev'n as He bade us, so we do.
Pray tell us, then, ye idlers, how
   He chanced to give the land to you.

We nestle close to Mother Earth—
   That mother whom ye hardly know;
If there be differing rights of birth,
   The higher rights are ours to show.

Ye own the land?   Then why not claim
   The air and sky and ocean broad?
Fill out the patents in your name;
   Your courts will soon condone the fraud.

The world is yours?   This globe that steers
   Through heaven her swift, mysterious way,
Shining among her sister spheres,
   In fact belongs to you, you say?

Oh, boast insane !   And if ye dare
   Evict us from earth's ample face,
Perhaps we'll find who holds out there
   The deeds to interstellar space.

And we may meet the owners, too,
   Of all the planets, great and small,
And trespassing on each anew,
   Descry no place for us at all.

The Workers to the Landlords

Nay, in the heaven ye deign to hold,
　　To quiet us, before our eyes,
Who knows but ye'll have bought and sold
　　The fields and glades of paradise?

Fools, blush at this your mad pretence,
　　To own God's everlasting land!
'Tis no more yours than ours, for hence
　　We draw our food, and here we stand.

The self-same path that brought you here,
　　That path by our feet too was worn.
Our right to live on earth is clear;
　　Our right is this, that we were born.

Learn from the birds.　And do they pay
　　Each other rent for oak and beech?
The fish that swim in creek and bay
　　Have a free nook to spawn for each.

And only we, the sons of men,
　　Without a resting-place are left;
While fowl and fox have nest and den.
　　The rent ye take from us is theft.

The poor man's wife has not a spot
　　Where she may bear her firstborn son;
Nor has he where to build his cot,
　　Or lay his bones when life is done.

New York at 99° in the Shade

A foothold here we now demand.
> The right to space we will not buy.
Do you repeat, " We own the land "?
Before Almighty God, you lie !

New York at 99° in the Shade ⚘

I

WALK with me down through the furnace-like
     street ;
Feel the hot paving-stones under your feet ;
Breathe the dead air ; smell the vile human smells ;
Don't lag behind though your stomach rebels.
Now it is night, and the sun has long set ;
Still how his rays seem to blister us yet.
Elbow your way through the sweltering mass.
Moist, pallid faces are turned as we pass.
Some are of men who have toiled all the day.
Children are screaming in dirt as they play ;
Woe-begone women, with babes at the breast,
Sit in the doorways unkempt and half dressed.
All talk at once ; the night passes in din.
Soon will the work of a new day begin.
Ah, 'tis enough to make angels despair ;
This is the thing they call taking the air !
Enter this hallway ; climb five flights of stairs ;
Visit the dens where the poor have their lairs,—

New York at 99° in the Shade

Kitchen and bedroom and parlour in one,
Cooking the life that was left by the sun,—
Windowless cupboards where men try to sleep,
Heedless of roaches and bugs as they creep.
Some burn with fever, and here they must die,
Crowded like litters of pigs in a sty.
One narrow house, rising floor above floor,
Holds a full hundred of mortals and more.
Up on a roof see a score or two lie,
Seeking for slumber beneath the dull sky.
Let us be proud of the city we've made,
After a day ninety-nine in the shade.

As I look up at the stars, lo, behold!
Comes to my ear, as to shepherds of old,
Strains as it were from a heavenly choir,
Singing, " O brothers who toil, never tire!
 Justice will come if you look for it higher."

II

Follow me now to the streets near the Park.
Palace and mansion loom up in the dark.
Windows are closed ; all the people have fled.
Surely this seems like a town of the dead.
Gone to the mountains or gone to the sea,
Travelling in Europe for two months or three ;
Here they have left in the heat and the gloom
Houses as empty of life as the tomb.

New York at 99° in the Shade

Come, I've a latch-key, let's go in and roam
Ghost-like through halls of what once was a home.
Look at the tables and pictures, and all
Covered each one like a corpse with its pall.
Beds of the softest invitingly stand,
Luxury wickedly cumbering the land.
Here, were the waifs of the slums to repose,
Soon they'd forget all their trials and woes.
Think what a blessing,—I say it with wrath,—
Could they but dip in this porcelain-lined bath.
Miles upon miles of such houses stretch forth,
Bolted and barred, from the south to the north.
Children may perish like flies in the heat,
How could we let them pollute a fine street?
Let us be proud of the city we've made,
After a day ninety-nine in the shade.

    Down on the curb again, what do I hear?
    Up from the sewer comes a song harsh and
        clear;
    List to the words of the devil's own choir,
    " Sodom, Gomorrah, with Sidon ánd Tyre,
    Wait for New York in the depths of hell-fire."

Song of the New Freedom ✍

(Tune, " Ein' Feste Burg.")

AMERICANS, ye once were free,
    Your country led the nations' van,
Proclaiming new-born liberty,
The lost self-sovereignty of man.
    All Europe then was glad
    To follow in your train.
    The glory that ye had
    Would ye once more regain?
Then know, ye trust your arms in vain.

In vain ye build your battle-ships,
In vain ye fortify the coast;
Still many an armament outstrips
The devilish frenzy of your boast.
    Think not to lead by force.
    Ever have men relied
    In vain on such a course.
    Be free and far and wide,
The world will rally to your side.

Be free. Ye brag of freedom yet;
But do ye not, while glorying, feel

Song of the New Freedom

The tightening bonds? Can ye forget
The fetters dragging at your heel?
  Each battle Freedom wins
  Transforms her foe of old.
  Another strife begins;
  A tyrant new behold—
The sullen, swinish god of gold.

Arise and strike the usurper down—
The basest of the despot brood.
Come, trample on his vulgar crown,
And let him welter in his blood.
  Where is he, do ye ask?
  Look not in street or mart.
  Within you find your task;
  He lords it in your heart.
There let the desperate conflict start.

Your heart is ruled by love of pelf;
Your land is ruled by pelf amassed.
Cast down the former; free yourself,
And soon you'll bind the latter fast.
  Hark to our country's call,
  And let us all unite;
  The tyrant soon will fall.
  Yea, as our cause is right,
Freedom again shall gain the fight!

A Good Job for the Flag ❧

SEE the old flag over the village school.
  What a fine idee ter h'ist him there.
He looks so big and calm and cool,
That somehow it clears the air.
    He's a-watchin' the girls and boys,
    As they squint at paper and pen ;
    Ur enjoyin' the playground's noise —
      The ball and the bat,
      Ur whatever they're at,
    And the makin' o' women and men.
I'd like ter bet that his hours don't drag.
Now that's what I call a good job fur a flag.

He's kinder reformed, as it seems ter me,
Fur he wunst was a rayther tough old case.
Bad company did it, as you might see,
When he loafed about the place,
    Hobnobbin' with bay'nets and guns,
    And pistols and swords and the like ;
    Turnin' the heads of our sons,
      Makin' 'em spile,
      Both the rank and the file,
    Fur a chance to shoot and strike,
Swellin' their noddles with bluster and brag.
Now that's what I call a mean job fur a flag.

156

Hereafter in Far Distant Years

The stars in the blue were fur pride, I said ;—
You jest should 'a' seen them young ones'
    airs ;
And bloodshed was meant by the stripes of
    red —
They'd have liked to kill if they dared.
    But we've changed all that right here.
    Stars of innocence speck the blue.
    If the red means blood, it's clear
      It's the blood that it oughter,
      That's thicker than water,
    Of brothers and sisters true.
Three cheers fur the law that made him wag
Way over the children, the good old flag.

Hereafter in Far Distant Years ✒

HEREAFTER, in far distant years,
    If this book, by some chance surviving, fall
into the hands of curious readers,
They will smile perplexed, and say :
" How strange that even in those barbarous times
It seemed worth while to write these simple, self-
    evident truths,
And solemnly to set forth such wisdom as now our
    babes are born with !

Surely there never was an age when things so
elementary were honestly gainsaid.
Oh, the mystery of eyes that see nct and ears that
hear not ! "

Somewhere 🙠

I'M sure that somewhere, I know not when,
   I lived very far from the haunts of men ;
         For still as a child,
         There was something wild
That thrilled my heart every now and then.

I'm sure that at sometime, I know not where,
I used to float, float, float through the air ;
         Because, when I dream,
         I so often seem
To be soaring demurely and safe up there.

Death 🙠

I

HAIL, cleansing, purifying Death !
   I see you as a pretty red-cheeked housemaid,
   with neat white cap and trim apron,

Death

Cheerily singing at your work, as you dust and clean
    and scrub the good old house of Life ;
Sweeping together the rubbish, and quietly putting it
    out at the door,
Where it will find new surroundings, and be no
    longer filth.
What could we do without you, poor, dirt-excreting,
    disease-breeding mortals that we are ?
What would become of us if we did not at last fall
    under your grateful ministrations ?
And who can tell how often we may have need of
    them ?

II

I wait for you, dear sister, confidently, fearlessly ;
I seem to recognise you.
I am half persuaded that I have met you before.
When you come toward me with your pail and soap
    and water, may your song be of the merriest.
I will not turn away from you.
You will lay hold of me firmly, but tenderly too, I
    am sure.
Who knows ?   Perhaps you may even kiss me on
    the forehead.

III

And in the hereafter how shall we look back at you,
    sister ?

In the Breakers

Will it not be as at a kindly, bustling, gossipy mid-
     wife,
Who ushered us into life, and was proud of our
     weight, and gave us our first bath, and put
     on the new clothes that were waiting for
     us ?

In the Breakers ~&

I

WHAT grand sport it is to dive under the
     breakers,
Measuring your lithe buoyancy against their im-
     petuous strength,
The gravitation that sinks the stone bearing you up,
     as you plunge through the solid green mass,
     following the sandy bottom just too long ;
Striking out upward madly in search of breath ;
Shooting like a rocket into the midst of the surging,
     struggling billows ;
Abandoning yourself to them like the seaweed,
     beaten hither and thither, your head turning
     in a boiling caldron, the water roaring in your
     ears, the salt in your eyes ;
At last bursting forth into the swelling stillness
     beyond the line of foam ;

In the Breakers

Basking idly on your back in the sun, looking
    sleepily, as you rock in your cradle, at the
    immense, unfathomable blue ;
Lulled by the thundering cadence on the shore, now
    so far, far away.

II

But while you were there under the seething surf,
What if you had forgotten the fresh air overhead
    and had made no effort to reach it, thinking
    that where you were there you ought to
    remain, and taking the salt water and the
    breathlessness as the necessary stuff of life ?
What would have become of your sport then, and
    how soon would your dead body have been
    swept out to the hungry sharks ?

III

In the world too we are often likewise submerged.
Over our heads the troubled waves of anxiety close,
    and we hardly remember that the sun is still
    shining.
Distracted with cares, drawn this way and that by
    desires, caught in a whirl of toil or business
    or pleasure or metaphysics ;
Forcing ourselves to believe that we are in our true
    element ;

The Living Answer

Weighing ourselves down till we no longer feel our
      native buoyancy;
Gasping for air, and thinking to find it under our
      feet,—
Ah, this is no sport.
Life is only a noble exercise so long as we bear in
      mind the sun and sky above us, and know
      enough to come up to the surface from time
      to time for breath.
Remember that, and the direst forces of nature
      become our friends and playthings.
Only remember, and what sport it is to be alive!

The Living Answer

WHERE is the answer to all the contradic-
      tions?—
The fact that things must happen as they do,
And my easy choice to do as I like?—
The lavish waste and destruction of nature,
And the infinite wisdom in which I seem to share?—
The fierce struggle for life,
And the peace which passeth all understanding?—
The pain and misery of man and beast,
And the almighty love whose rays I feel?—
Death everywhere, and yet life eternal somehow

swelling into all the nooks and corners without driving it out?—
Good ruling over evil triumphant?
Where is the answer?

Every age has its futile philosopher with his scheme, explaining one side perhaps but blind to the other.
Every age buries the philosophy of its predecessor, until now the churchyard is full of dead answers.
There is but one living answer.
I am that answer;—
I, with my free will bound up in destiny;
I, with my prodigality and thrift;
I, so stormy on the surface and yet with unsounded depths of calm beneath;
I, with my sorrow and joy, my love and hate, my sympathy and my cruelty;
I, going down to death and yet for ever living;
I, with right and wrong fighting their endless duel within me.
In me the contradictions are reconciled.
Yes; I, who transcend all philosophies, who refuse to be imprisoned by theories and systems, who elude all logic, and have no bounds but Eternity.
I am the answer.

Rabboni ut Videamus ❧

OPEN our eyes, O Lord,
   Who wander in the night.
One blessing to Thy Church accord—
   That it receive its sight.

Show us the world we make—
   This world of crime and pain ;
Show us the want from which we take
   Our fill of cruel gain.

Show us the clear effect
   Of every thought and deed ;
Make it so easy to detect,
   That he that runs may read.

Like us, our fathers groped ;
   Their eyes were holden too ;
While they adored and prayed and hoped,
   They lived as tyrants do.

They could not see the slave
   Oppressed and scourged and bound ;
They could not see the look he gave
   For help he never found.

Nor did their eyes behold
    The horror of their laws,
Which hanged and burned both young and old
    For every trivial cause.

And they who were the first
    To point them out their sin,
Were mobbed, imprisoned, hated, cursed,
    And killed by kith and kin.

O Lord, vouchsafe Thy grace,
    That when again Thou send
A messenger before Thy face,
    We greet him as a friend.

And may we with him dare
    To choose the eternal right;
But grant us first our fervent prayer—
    That we receive our sight!

Mother Nature

DEAR Mother Nature, let us be reconciled!
    How long it is since we were on speaking
    terms!
I have been sulking, and I thought you were sulking
    too.

The Vision of the Pioneers

I wanted you to come and make up, but I see that I
　　was in the wrong, and that I must take the
　　first step.
I believed all the stories that I heard about you, and,
　　to tell the truth, I looked upon you as a rather
　　questionable character.
In vain I tried to compass your exuberance with my
　　yard-stick.
Your prodigality and indecency and recklessness
　　shocked me beyond measure.
How could I afford to be seen in such company?

But I perceive more clearly now.
There, I have broken my yard-stick across my knee,
　　and thrown away the pieces.
It will never come between us again.
I know now that you are just what you ought to be,
　　and I would not have you other than you are.
Forgive me, Mother, and take me back to your
　　bosom!

The Vision of the Pioneers 🕭

I SAW the Angel of the New Truth with the
　infant Time that is to be in her arms.
Oh, how the great pioneers had to struggle before
　　they gained the point of vantage whence they
　　could see that vision,

The Bonds of Freedom

For weary years pushing though the darksome forest,
    their minds haunted with the memory of the
    radiant hem of her garment, of which erewhile
    they had caught a vanishing glimpse.
And I, following afar off, had my adventures too ;
The thickets still were full of brambles, and the wild
    beasts had not yet ceased to prowl.
But soon the path will be well trodden down, and a
    broad highway will at last be opened for the
    onward pressing peoples.
When the babe is weaned, the angel will return to
    heaven.
Forget the pioneers, if you will.
What matters it ? They have had their reward, for
    they saw the vision at its brightest.

The Bonds of Freedom ❧

FREEDOM, dear tyrant, how little I understood
    you!
Did I expect to have a rollicking, easy life with
    you ?
Ah, it is only irresponsible slaves that can live thus.
Your path is narrow and steep, and now a necessity
    tenfold heavier than before impels me onward.
No longer may I look to the right hand nor to the
    left.

The Kingdom of God

I see the illusion of my free will, and the folly of
   praying, "My will be done."
And yet, while I behold that patch of blue sky above
   me, and feel the wind of heaven blowing down
   the mountain pass, even though all mankind
   spread themselves over the plains beneath the
   clouds with their faces to the ground, I know
   that I and such as I alone are free.

The Kingdom of God 🕭

WHAT is the kingdom of God?
      Is it a far-away singing of psalms and
      harping of harps?
Or a new order here on earth introduced by act of
   the legislature, and enforced by Courts and
   policemen?
Or a mad revel of licence, with each man's desire a
   law unto itself?

Nay, the kingdom of God is that social life which
   expresses man's realisation of the divine consciousness within him.
In this consciousness behold the Christ come down
   to save the world,—
God manifest in the flesh, and for ever persecuted
   and crucified,

Descending with His life-line to the lowest depths
    of creation,
And rising at last again to the throne, having drawn
    all things unto Himself.
This is the eternal fact of the creeds, the drama of
    history, the kingdom of God.

Dear Old England ❧

DEAR old England, how I hate
    All the things that make you great!
Still I cannot but declare
My love for all that keeps you fair.

I've no patience with the steam,
That makes your factory-whistles scream;
With your machines and with your coal,
Blackening body, mind, and soul.

Neither can I stand the slums
Whence your starving workman comes,
And where, beneath a smoky pall,
He rarely sees the sun at all.

Think you Englishmen were made
To be sacrificed to Trade?
More romantic butcheries
Were the Druids' 'neath the trees.

Dear Old England

On these sights I turn my back.
Lo, fields of green, not towns of black;
Skies of blue, not clouds of smoke;
And stalwart, red-cheeked village folk.

There the cottage, calm and still,
Nestles down beside the hill,
And lane and hedge and ancient beech
Seem just created each for each.

See the dairymaid await
Her lover at the garden gate,
While an apocalypse of green
Transfigures all the tidy scene.

Wherefore flee from fields and downs,
Crowding into ugly towns?
Wherefore plough the distant main?
What, have you sold your souls to Gain?

'Tis a low, ignoble quest,
Seeking markets east and west!
Better that your flag were furled,
Than forcing gimcracks on the world.

Stop your melancholy wars,
Wherein you win no glorious scars.
Learn at last, if you are able,
That Profit is unprofitable.

Dear Old England

Call back home your wandering sons
With their Testaments and guns.
Whither are their footsteps bent?
Here they might have found content.

Here they have at their own price
The making of a paradise.
Nowhere will they find a stage
So fitted for the Golden Age.

You've spread your empire out too thin
With greed and violence and sin;
Now let a stabler reign commence,
Deeper, more lofty, more intense.

Search for justice, not for gold.
Boundless wealth your islands hold.
Silver's but a doubtful good.
Come, work the mines of brotherhood.

Then at last—but who can tell
Such miracles as ne'er befell?—
Then England will be great indeed,
And all the world will cry, " God-speed."

Dear old England, how I hate
The things that now have made you great!
Still I love you, for I see
Your greatness that is bound to be.

√ **America Libera** ❧

America Libera

QUOTH America:
    "Would you confine me, with my
vigorous, exuberant life, in your
constitutions and statutes?

Little do you know me.

No sooner have your masons finished my prison-
house, than I walk out at the door.

Though the lodging suit me to-day, I shall need
wider scope to-morrow.

Tinker at it as you will; patch it and piece it out
from dawn till eventide; you are working at
an empty shell; I have already escaped and
eluded you.

While you plod along at the old edifice, I am filling
my lungs out of doors.

None of your tailors can make me raiment which I
shall not outgrow in a fortnight.

While I slept, you might fasten your Lilliputian
threads around me, but when I rise I do not
even hear them when they snap asunder.

All your handicraftsmen cannot keep up with my
life.

I am alive and growing apace, and you treat me as
if I were dead.

If your contrivances should fit me now like a tortoiseshell, I should still shed them at the end of the year.

Only in my coffin shall I rest quietly, like another China or Turkey, and accept passively your well-meant attentions.

Meanwhile unhand me, ye mummy-makers, for I am alive."

The Lighthouse ❧

I

IT is a glorious day at sea.

Our steamer is plunging proudly through the waves like a happy monster.

The porpoises playing round her nose do not make our mistake of taking her for a mere lifeless thing.

They recognise a fellow-creature, and tease her as fox-terrier puppies tease a mastiff; but she shakes them off and ploughs ahead.

Our group on the port-bow, however, and all the other groups gazing over the port-rail, have minds fixed on something else than the ship.

For a week or more our thoughts have been im-prisoned in the little world of the ship's

The Lighthouse

company, with its narrow interests and small-talk.

Our miniature community shaped itself for a time with the natural inevitableness of chemical affinity, but now that has all passed away.

A suggestion, a new idea, has hopelessly disturbed the molecules, and they are already on the lookout for more powerful forces and a more comprehensive arrangement.

The man at the mast-head has sighted the Lizard light, and we are straining our eyes to obtain a glimpse of it.

The starboard deck is quite deserted, but on this side all is wide awake, as if our leviathan were swimming with one eye open.

We stare impatiently until our eyes ache, but nothing is visible except the green sea and the sunny, wind-driven foam, and behind, the endless sweep of the clear sky.

That unseen lighthouse has, without our knowing it, changed all our relations to each other, and we are unconsciously adjusting ourselves to new centres.

The doom of our tiny social system of a week, with its hierarchy and traditions, has been irrevocably pronounced.

At last a sharp-eyed boy cries out, "There it is!" and with varying degrees of truth we chime in.

But is it really the lighthouse, or the white edge of
a cloud lit up by the declining sun, or an
illusion of our sight?

Now, just before sunset, all doubt ceases, for the
white elusive speck has given place to a star,
come down to do sentinel duty for us all
night on the distant coast.

We go below to dinner, but we are no longer the
same men and women that breakfasted
together, and we are half aware that we
have grown.

II

God bless the lighthouses of life—the men whose
feet are on the rock, and who stand as pillars
of cloud by day and pillars of fire by night, to
mark our course to the promised land.

Who would not be such a lighthouse?

Ah, that ambition I have never altogether scotched.

The others died hard, but they died, and as I was
congratulating myself that I was cured of
castle-building for good and all, this new ideal
rose up from the ashes of the rest mightier
than any of them.

In vain I admonish my soul, and say, "Live now,
in the present, for sufficient unto the day is
the good thereof, and the morrow will take
thought of the things of itself."

Love's Blindness

It is of no use; the fight within me is still on,
    and I still long to serve as the Lizard light,
    drawing other voyagers on the eternal ocean
    from their petty, ephemeral worlds.

Love's Blindness

LOVE is blind? Oh, miraculous blindness,
    Whose insight is touched from above
With the zest of divine loving-kindness !
He sees best who is deepest in love.

Competition

DO you fear competition?
    Fear it not, for it is Nature's way, and it
    is foolish to think that we know a better.
What is competition but the triumph of the
    mightiest?
If God is almighty, of whom shall we be afraid?
If love is the greatest of all forces, who can presume
    to stand against us?

The quiet-burning sun lifts up the waters and pours
    them over Niagara;

He calls forth the winds and marshals the thunder-
clouds;
At his bidding the cyclone cuts a swathe through
the forest, and the tornado lashes the sea to
frenzy.
When the sun is submerged in the cataract,—
When he is blown hither and thither by the
tempest,—
Then, and not till then, fear competition.

High Mass ❧

THE brocaded and velveted priest raises the
host in the sight of the congregation.
The silver bell tinkles, and the people, kneeling on
their handkerchiefs upon the paved floor,
cross themselves and worship.
And I, who have long since done with temples and
proceeded onward, I, too, worship with them.
I am as sure that God is there as they are.

As I kneel, the scene changes.
It is the Israelitish High Priest in his white linen
garments who now stands at the altar.
He passes within the veil, swinging a smoking
censer, and the air is full of the smell of
incense.

High Mass

We are all waiting in the outer court, and we
    tremble as we see the fiery Shekinah through
    his eyes.
I see it as plainly as if it burned before me.

The smoke from the censer hides everything, and
    again there is a change of scene.
We are in an Egyptian temple.
The fruits of the earth have been laid symmetrically
    upon the altar.
The priest with outstretched arms is offering them
    to Osiris.
On each side stiff, impassive Egyptians in like
    manner hold forth their upturned hands.
I join with the crowd in weeping for Osiris slain
    and in rejoicing for him risen again.

The people are rising from their knees, and we are
    in church once more.
I am not out of place here, for I am more catholic
    than any of them.
I can adore with Jew and Mohammedan and
    Pagan.
My religion shuts out none of the faithful in any
    age or any clime.
There are many roads to God, for He is latent
    everywhere.

Magnets

Upon whatever point the faith of men converges
and focuses itself, there the divine spark
flames up.
They that seek it find it, and where two or three
are gathered together in its name, there it is
in the midst of them.

Magnets

TWO chubby, curly-headed children, brother
and sister, are sitting on the floor, on each
side of a basin of water.
They are bending over it intently, as they amuse
themselves by drawing tiny tin boats about
their miniature sea with a pair of magnets.
They never tire of watching the sensitive bowsprits,
which yield themselves like the antennæ of
insects to the unseen power.
The boy, by some awkward motion, upsets one of
the little vessels;
His sister looks up, their eyes meet, and they both
burst into merry laughter.
Then the girl impulsively throws her arms about
his neck and kisses him, at imminent peril of
a plunge in the deep and the annihilation of
the entire fleet.

Magnets

What infinite, mysterious forces the divine little
    animals are thoughtlessly playing with, as
    they attract the boats with their magic wands,
    and draw each other kiss-wards with their
    eyes !
Are these two forces distinct, or do they not rather
    merge into one ?
I shall not presume to separate them—I, who feel
    my heart tremble within me like the needle
    in the compass, often shaken out of place
    and pointing wrong, but ever quivering back
    again, moved by some great, unknown, un-
    thinkable influence.
On the boisterous sea, with the horizon broken and
    the stars themselves ever passing in proces-
    sion, there is nothing so stable as the rest-
    less needle and the restless soul.
Yes, they are akin each to each, and swayed by
    kindred powers ;
And it is one and the same game that the children
    are playing together.

The Reformer ❧

THE Reformer stood in the market-place with his arms folded.

He smiled on the angry mob surging round him, because he knew that he bore that within him which they could not kill.

The Angel of Truth sat secure in his heart, and feared not, for she felt that her fortress was impregnable.

Let them torture and mutilate and murder, her, at least, they could not touch.

One taunt too bitter, one cry too shrill pierced the ear of the hunted man.

He frowned and clenched his fist.

A shadow passed over his soul, and the angel turned deathly pale.

Then he lifted his arm and struck his nearest assailant full in the face, and the angel flew slowly from her tottering stronghold up to heaven.

That night the world was poorer and emptier, but the Angel of Truth still bides her time.

The State 🐛

The State

I

THEY talked much of the State—the State.

I had never seen the State, and I asked them to picture it to me, as my gross mind could not follow their subtle language when they spake of it.

Then they told me to think of it as of a beautiful goddess, enthroned and sceptred, benignly caring for her children.

But for some reason I was not satisfied.

And once upon a time, as I was lying awake at night and thinking, I had as it were a vision,

And I seemed to see a barren ridge of sand beneath a lurid sky;

And lo, against the sky stood out in bold relief a black scaffold and gallows-tree, and from the end of its gaunt arm hung, limp and motionless, a shadowy, empty noose.

And a Voice whispered in my ear, "Behold the State incarnate!"

And as I looked aghast, the desert became thickly peopled, and all the countless throng did obeisance to the gibbet;

And they that were clad in rich raiment bowed
down the lowest of all.

II

The Sheriff is reading his warrant to the condemned
man in his cell.
He stammers and hesitates, and his voice is husky.
The executioner takes off his victim's collar and
unbuttons his shirt, while the unhappy man
smooths down his new black coat with
twitching fingers, and watches the Sheriff's
fat hands, and wonders whether he can get
his gold ring off his little finger or not.
Now his hands are tied behind him, and the procession moves.
There is the doctor, the soldier of life, turned
deserter, and serving in the army of death.
There is the priest, holding out hopes, in an under-
tone, of another world, where the inhabitants
are less inhuman than in this.
There are the correspondents of the press, eager for
any news that will sell.
The majesty of the law leads and brings up the
rear — the Sheriff and his deputies, the
attorneys and the police.
All that is respected in the community is represented
here.

The State

They have congregated like vultures scenting carrion
from afar.

The doomed man has braced himself up for a
supreme effort, but his knees are unsteady,
his underlip quivers, and his face is livid.

In these last weeks he has died a thousand deaths,
and his mind has suffered every kind of
torment.

How often has he gone through this scene before,
and yet how different it is—so much more
trivial and usual, and yet so much more
dreadful.

The ordinary words, " Good-morning," and " Thank
you," sound like a foreign language, and
still the day strangely resembles other
days.

As we turn a corner in the jail yard, and the
frightful hanging-machine appears, he averts
his eyes, and stumbles and nearly falls.

At last he is in place, the black cap is pulled over
his face and the noose adjusted.

The Sheriff drops his handkerchief, the floor gives
way with a creak—there is a sickening jerk,
and the rope stretches taut ;

Then after some minutes of convulsive struggle, that
seem like years, all is quiet.

The doctor comes forward and feels the dying man's
pulse.

He nods his head, and the little crowd disperses,
while four men lower the body into a box.

There was not one man in that company but felt
that something awful was happening which
ought not to happen ;—

Not one who did not know that the punishment was
infinitely more devilish than the crime ;—

Not one who at the bottom of his heart believed in
his right or in anyone else's right to dispose
of the life of his fellow-man, and trifle thus
with the mystery of death.

Yet with inexorable precision they went on to the
end.

Even the felon himself accepted the inevitable, and
never in all his talks with his confessor did
he think of asking how forgiveness and love
of neighbours and enemies was consistent
with all this.

What was it that urged them relentlessly on ?

When the Sheriff's little boy climbs on his knee in
the evening, and hides his face against the
breast of his coat, and says, " Father, why did
you do it ? " what will he answer?

Was it fate and destiny, or divine justice ?

Or was it not rather a poor, human make-shift
for these — a necessity, a justice of the
imagination ?

The State

" Don't cry, my child ; you cannot understand now,
    but I am a servant of the State, and must do
    as the State directs."
The State ?
Ah, thus it is that men conjure up spectres out of
    nothingness, and name them, and cast their
    sins upon them, and fall down and worship
    them.

III

I feel the force stirring within me which in time
    will re-form the world.
It does not push or obtrude, but I am conscious of
    it drawing gently and irresistibly at my vitals.
And I see that as I am attracted, so I begin
    unaccountably to attract others.
I draw them and they in turn draw me, and we
    recognise a tendency to group ourselves
    anew.
Get in touch with the great central magnet, and you
    will yourself become a magnet ;
And as more and more of us find our bearings and
    exert our powers, gradually the new world
    will take shape.
We become indeed legislators of the divine law,
    receiving it from God Himself in the Mount,
    and human laws shrivel and dry up before
    us.

And I asked the force within my soul, "Who art thou?"

And it answered and said, "I am Love, the Lord of Heaven, and I would be called Love, the Lord of Earth.

I am the mightiest of all the heavenly hosts, and I am come to create the State that is to be."

Postscript

It is not I that have written ;
 It is not I that have sung.
I'm the chord that Another has smitten, –
 The chime that Another has rung.

Do not blame me, for how can a man turn,
 And leave unrecorded behind
The truths which the great Magic Lantern
 Flashed bright on the blank of his mind.

I give but the things I am given ;
 I show but the things that I see ;
I draw, but my pencil is driven
 By a Force that is master of me.